Journey OM

A Soul Journeyer's Adventure

BOOK I OF THE JOURNEY OM SERIES

Shima Shanti

Journey OM
A Soul Journeyer's Adventure

Text Design by J.K. Eckert & Company
Photography by Jim Kelly
Edited by Teresa Brady
Cover Design by Mike Clark
Cover Illustration by James Gordon Kelly

ISBN: 978-0-9915481-2-5
LCCN: 2014909393

Printed in the United States of America
Second Printing June 2014
Lightning Source Printers

Published by
Peace Waters Publishing
San Diego, CA 92128
www.peacewaters.com

Printed in the United States of America

To Scout,

In All Ways I share Peace with you, my beloved husband.
You are the tether allowing me to soar in the celestial realms.

The wave and the moon will always be,
But the force between them will never be,
As strong as the Love between you and me.

Contents

James
She asked
Is the car gassed?
I responded
Yes, My Love

And wondering
I asked
Are we going for a ride?
She responded
Yes, My Love

And where are we going to go?
I asked
She responded
I don't know
But we'll have all our lives to get there.

—Jim Kelly

Starting Out

This is a "Once Upon A Time" story—once upon a time 10,000 years ago; once upon a time in 1877; and once upon a time in May 2009. It reads as fictional adventure, but it is non-fiction. Everything happened to me. It is a chronicle, a journey, a journal, a true adventure. In this story, time is not as we know it. Nature is not as we perceive it. It is a story to take or leave. If you travel to this journey's end, following the treasures Stargate to Stargate as we did, you can be sure it will expand your consciousness. It will touch you in some way, 10,000 years ago, in 1877 and/or Now.

Reading this journey will connect you energetically. You will share all of our experiences, receive all the benefits of all the lessons we learned simply by viewing and listening. You don't need to physically take the pilgrimage. We have done that for you. And that is our gift. From the Pleiadian Emissaries of Light, from Chief Joseph and the Nez Perce, from the Ascended Master Beings, the Planetary Kingdoms, animal and bird, plant and mineral, and from the One, Source of All, we invite you to "Journey On." Teleporting not required!

This book is written on two levels requiring passage through both the Earth grids and the Spiritual grids. For some it will be another interesting book of fictional adventure. For those who are ready, there are Spiritual lessons and Universal Truths direct from the Ascended Masters. Divine Light language has been presented to me, encoded by Sanat Kumara and Lady Venus. It is not one pen but a multitude of those who promised to bring the new teachings to Earth. My contribution is to fill-in the third dimension story about the Stargate journey; to keep you interested and the ego occupied and entertained while the genuine value of this book is the truths of Wisdom and the interactive Light and Love it transmits. It is authentic, pure. Archangel Gabriel is the Messenger; he seeds my energy pattern to keep me going with inspiration. While reading this book, know that it is Archangel Gabriel who assisted in publishing and moving this energy through the world systems to get it to you.

Chief Joseph

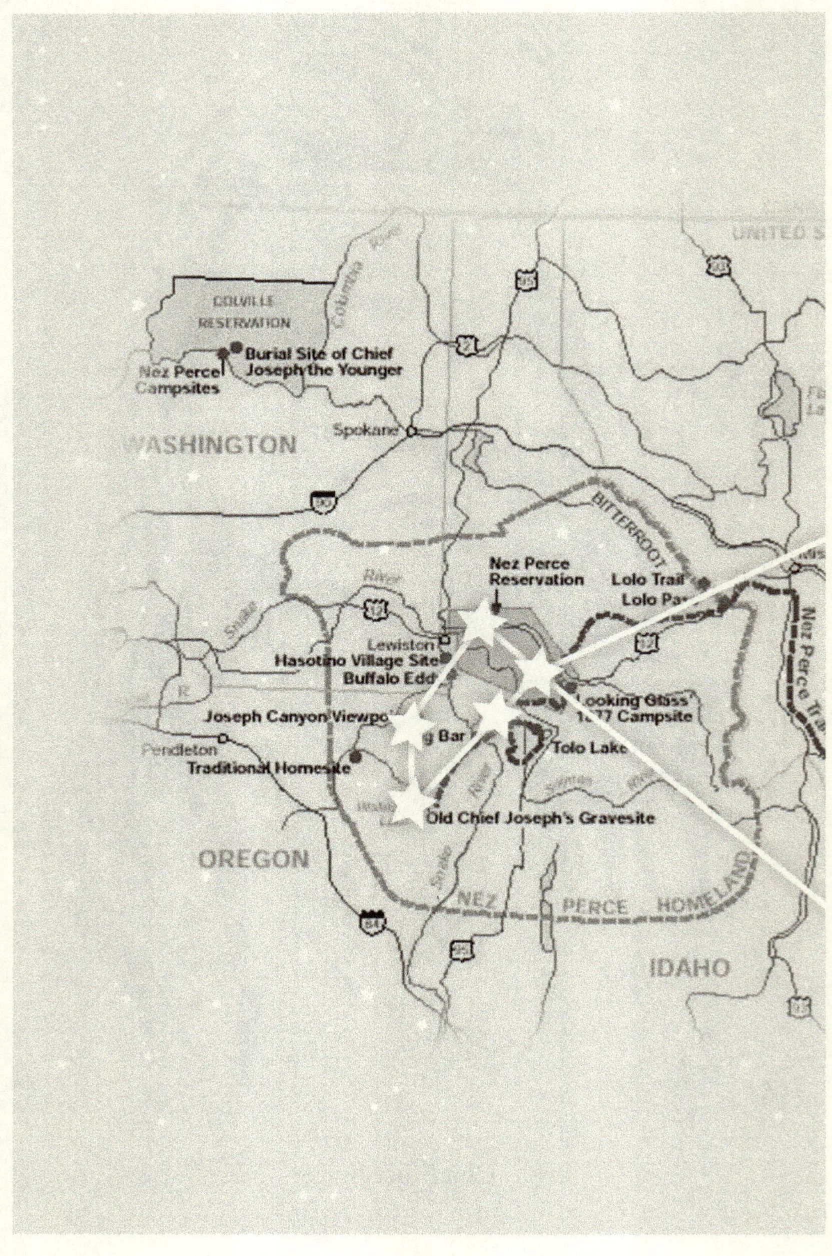
COLVILLE
RESERVATION
Burial Site of Chief
Joseph the Younger
Nez Perce
Campsites
WASHINGTON
Spokane
BITTERROOT
Nez Perce
Reservation
Lolo Trail
Lewiston
Hasotino Village Site
Looking Glass
1877 Campsite
Joseph Canyon Viewpo
Pendleton
Tolo Lake
Traditional Homesite
Old Chief Joseph's Gravesite
OREGON
NEZ PERCE HOMELAND
IDAHO

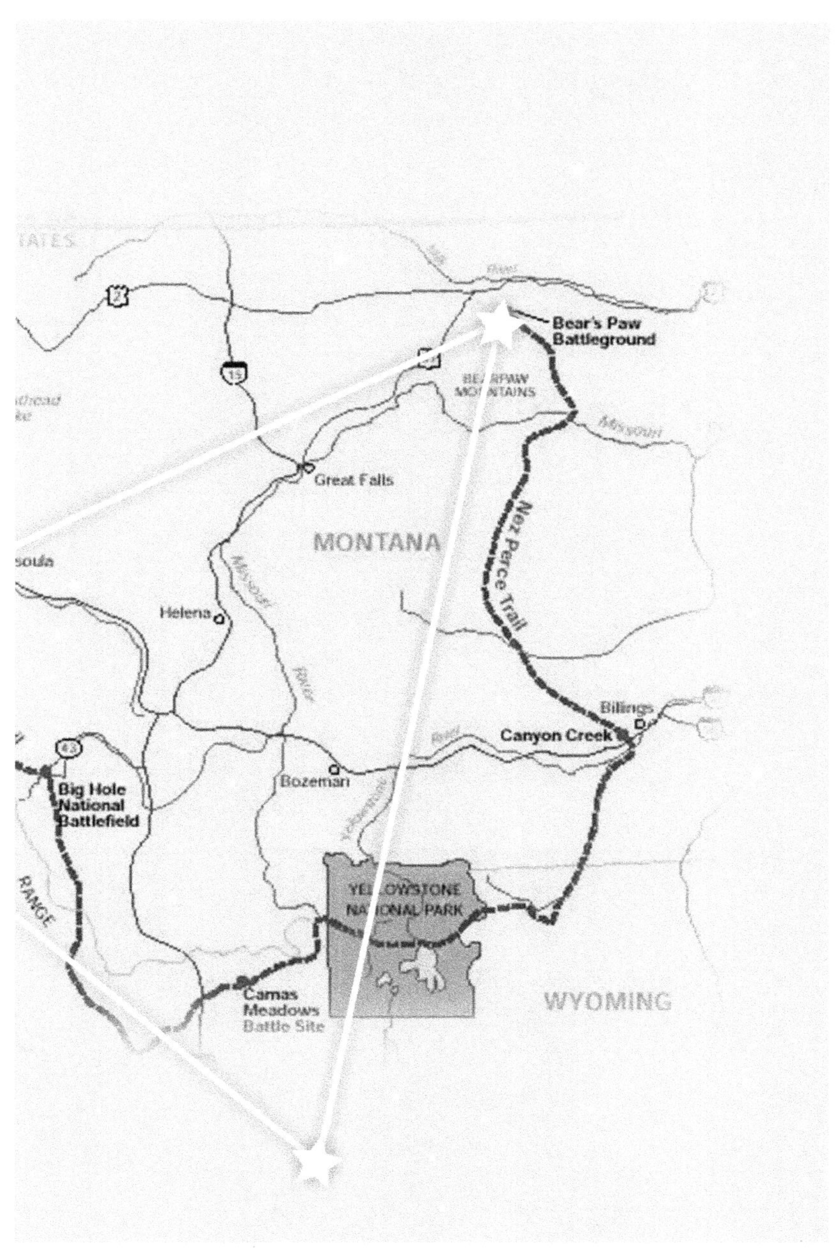
Bear's Paw
Battleground
BEARPAW
MOUNTAINS
Missouri
Great Falls
MONTANA
Nez Perce Trail
Helena
Billings
Canyon Creek
Bozeman
Big Hole
National
Battlefield
RANGE
YELLOWSTONE
NATIONAL PARK
Camas
Meadows
Battle Site
WYOMING

Waiting for the Tap on the Shoulder

My "God work" began in earnest in September 2007. Having been laid off from my latest sales job, I knew 25 years in corporate America had come to a close. Our son Jimmy, soon to be married, would be starting his new life with his beautiful bride, Liz. My life lay ahead like a blank canvas. I realized my original contracts were complete. I was ready for what I knew would be ascension or perhaps my next assignment from God. I bided my time gardening, walking on the beach, communing with angels in the loft, traveling back and forth between Whitefish, Montana and San Diego, California, enjoying the company of my husband.

I am content; peaceful. There is nothing more to resolve, to clear, or to correct. I am in love with my Self and in this state of grace ready to receive God's "tap on the shoulder" when

He will ask me to serve. I know my karma is complete and if I stay the course I won't incur new karma for the rest of my time on Earth.

Jim's and my love is steady, strong and sublime. For awhile now I have been coaxing him into thinking it won't last forever; that I would soon be on my way, probably by 2012. He takes it in stride, but I can feel the pain in his heart if he is to believe me and think it true. His "Skippy the Skeptic" attitude is his protection. Skippy wouldn't allow him to think I could "know" when I would leave the planet. Poetry is flowing from his heart at the thought of life without me.

God would never cause disharmony or loss for the sake of His Love. I had forgotten the lesson I learned years ago when I was chided by a spiritual teacher to choose God or Jim. No, there was never any question. I would always choose God, but I didn't think it was one or the other. At the time I believed if that was the requirement, I would choose God. I nearly did until Archangel Michael stepped in and said, "No, this isn't how God works." And in that moment I chose God by choosing Jim and my spiritual calling began in earnest. Deep within I knew Jim and I were not complete. It would be hard to imagine our love moving beyond what we already knew. Boy, did I underestimate God on this one!

On April 23, 2009, the tap came. I received a message from Chief Joseph as channeled by Judith:

My beloved sister, "Waneen Wan Yan," this is your name from 10,000 years ago when together we journeyed in a great migration pattern through the Pleiadian realms to Mother Earth as Emissaries of Light to seed the Nez Perce lineage. Ten thousand years ago the Arcturian Bear clan who had already followed the migration routes to this place met us when we descended from the Light ships. This was the blending of these two cosmic lineages that formed the Legions of Light of the Nez Perce, the Shoshone and the Southern Ute.

I AM Chief Joseph. I am of many bodies, but one soul. I AM Joseph your brother. I AM an immortal. For many lifetimes we have lived together as one with the natural world on this planet and other living green planets in the conscious vibration where life is sustainable. I knew when the killing times came, when my people could no longer live in Peace that you and I had to walk the pathway through the states of Idaho, Wyoming and Montana to make a living pathway of Light from Earth to the Pleiades. I have given my life that future generations may live. I chose Peace. I chose not to continue the ways of the warrior. I chose Peace that day. You witnessed my surrender.

You, my beloved sister are a messenger of the Morning Star who carries the keys to open the Stargates along this path which was marked as my exodus. On this trail you will open an ascension temple, Stargates that are of the cosmic order and the earthly plane. You have come into this lifetime as you have, not as a native and indigenous person because then you would have the wounds of your people to be healed. You must be fully ascended and fully in your ascension Light Body to open these Cosmic Christ Stargates.

When you make this pilgrimage, you will be shown the places to open the Stargates. It is important for you to learn and speak your name, Waneen Wan Yan, for the vibration opens the Stargates. Once they are opened you will return to San Diego to anchor and ground the Pleiadian Christ star codes in this anti-gravity field. May 25th *is the date that I can give you now.*

You will come to the place where before we surrendered you left your sacred bundle. You will know the place. It will be close to the proximity where I surrendered. There you will touch the sacred grandmother stone and your medicine ways will return through you to the people. I will be fully present in my immortal being and will initiate you in the medicine way of the Lodge of Peace. This is the promise made to you when you open the Cosmic Christ Stargates.

Many spirits will be walking with you on this pilgrimage. They are Wisdom Keepers. You know them. They are your Ancestors. You must bring their souls back into the world from the places they went when the doors to the portals were closed. When they return they will travel with you on my trail. You will meet others in the form of helpers on the pathway, humans who have agreed to help you. They all are waiting for you to make this pilgrimage. 2009 is the year.

For you know you are a Gateway of Light. I am happy to be with you. It is a good reunion. It is a good time to come home. I

AM Joseph, Chief of the Nez Perce people from the beginning of time and the beginning of this nation. I came as the Chief of these people. You came as my sister. It is good that we are together again. My heart is very happy because my relatives and ancestors, those who are yet to come to the Earth and those who came before, through this gift will have a meeting point of the souls. That which was wounded in the past can heal. And this proud lineage who were gifted the future of Peace, will be again, not as warriors, but as Peace Keepers as we were before we were forced to defend our land.

Oh the richness, the beauty, the sweetness of the rivers filled with salmon once again. The berries ripe and plump upon the bushes in the fall harvest. And the bear grease given and not taken by Grandmother Bear. My spirit still soars as an Eagle in the sacred land of Chief Joseph's path. Aho. I have spoken.

Over the last two years I had many "God job" opportunities offered to me through channeling with Judith. Some I recognized as mine to complete and others I politely declined. I knew one of my assignments was the Ascension Keys, a pure gift from God to work in the vibrations of Light Language. They manifest seamlessly and timelessly.

But this one—I'm just not so sure. I am being asked to go on a pilgrimage. When I think of pilgrimages I think of Jerusalem, Spain, Fatima, Lourdes, foreign countries unknown to me and difficult to navigate. Yes, it sounds intriguing.

Yes, I get tingles all over as Chief Joseph is speaking. Yes, travel is always fun, but in this lifetime I have not had a connection with the Native American cultures. They are unfamiliar to me, although I respect and honor their reverence to Mother Earth. My comfort zone is in the celestial realms. Grounding has always been lacking for me and the indigenous people represent to me the essence of grounding to Mother Earth. Ascension has been my desire for as long as I can remember, leaving planet Earth, going back to the age of three.

And yet, there were so many things in alignment that *did* make sense to me. I knew the Pleiades to be one of my homes and my most recent spiritual heritage before incarnating on Earth during the time of Lemuria when I came from Venus to seed the vibration of Love. Ten thousand years ago it was the Pleiadians who seeded the Nez Perce tribe with Peace. I could have easily been one of those Emissaries of Light. I know I have had many incarnations as a medicine woman and shaman. The one I am most familiar with is the Ute tribe of Southern Utah, very close to the Nez Perce.

And there was the fact that this pilgrimage was practically in my back yard. I grew up in Montana. I knew the Pacific Northwest and the West. I was comfortable in this land. We own a house in Whitefish and we store a car there for use when we visit. I had no time constraints. I was retired. I could come and go as I pleased. If it took weeks, fine. If it took months I could do that too. I was comfortable with the thought of traveling alone. It would be way too much to ask Jim to accompany me if it involved a large chunk of time. But God had that taken care of that too. I knew I had already said "Yes" on a subconscious level. Chief Joseph was just bringing me up to date and my departure was imminent.

Coincidentally, when I received this request to open Stargates we already had a trip planned to Whitefish, Montana for May 22nd. We'd already planned to take the car for service to Spokane which wasn't too far from the origination point of Chief Joseph's trail. It would take a week for the service repairs, during which time we would have a loaner car. We could use that for our pilgrimage and return to pick up our car at the end of our travels.

So I listened with openness. I have learned on my spiritual path to say "Yes." If it is not meant to be it will simply fall away. If it is my calling there is no stopping it! But first and foremost, I must be open and willing to be of service. Willingness is the gift I have and cherish. I have no problem volunteering. Discernment is my challenge. Funny, as I think about it, I use discernment best with things I am supposed to do. I was using a lot of discernment with this!

I sat with it. I resonated with Chief Joseph's message. He spoke to my heart. I learned that Chief Joseph is one of the incarnations of Ascended Master St. Germain. I had been working closely with St. Germain over the last year, with the Violet Flame, the Atomic Accelerator and the Ascension ceremonies. I understood the dedication and magnificence of his service to our planet.

St. Germain is one of the most selfless and giving of the Ascended Masters. After his ascension he received dispensation to return in physical form to continue his work on our behalf. There is no greater Love. His works could fill this entire book. His endeavors to free mankind date back 70,000 years. Since then he has re-embodied many times too numerous to mention to assist us in our evolution.

One of St. Germain's many incarnations included Saint Joseph the protector and husband of Mother Mary and guardian of Jesus. He also embodied as Merlin the great alchemist, and Christopher Columbus. He was Francis Bacon the English philosopher and the writer credited for composing the plays of William Shakespeare. He was known as the Comte de Saint Germain, a miraculous person of great wealth who dazzled the courts of 18th and 19th century Europe. As the Comte he used his incredible influence as a means of effecting change in bringing about greater harmony and cooperation between the nations of Europe. He helped in the drafting of the Declaration of Independence.

There is no brief, easy way to express the supreme Love St. Germain has for mankind. It was he and Lady Nada who petitioned and received dispensation from the Karmic Board to bring spiritual instruction to the masses in a straightforward format rather than veiled in mysticism. This direct communication opened the gates to our spiritual evolution and was truly the beginning of the New Age. He is the Chohan (Lord) of the Seventh Ray, the Violet Flame of Transmutation. The Violet Flame is probably the greatest gift given to mankind. When we invoke the Violet Flame all misqualified energy every miscreated by us in all time, space and dimension, knowingly or unknowingly, is instantly transmuted. In past times the only way to transmute our miscreations was through karma. The Violet Flame eliminates this requirement. It is a most precious gift to us, just for the asking. Learn about the Violet Flame and use it in your daily life. You (and I) will be forever blessed.

St. Germain reincarnated in 1877 as Chief Joseph to complete this very important soul contract for mankind. Needless to say, I would happily be of service to St. Germain—no questions asked.[1] I knew it was St. Germain embodied as Chief Joseph who would guide me on this Stargate Pilgrimage, that Germain would be leading me down this adventurous path. I had some experience with opening Stargates, although at the time I didn't know what I was doing. In fact, on April 23, 2009 I didn't even know what a Stargate was—so I googled.

What is a Stargate?

A Stargate is an etheric interdimensional energy alignment between two points in interstellar space. Stargate energies

[1] St. Germain is the Chohan of the 7th Ray. His domain is to watch who is bringing in the energy and who is capable of its speediest transition, then to assist those who are ready to match up with the energy of the Master that is giving it. When their time is right and their bodies are ready he implements the energy. This is how Divine manifestation occurs in its purest form. We are incredibly blessed by the selfless Love and assistance so freely given to us by those who have gone before, the Ascended Masters.

accelerate the integration of higher dimensions into the etheric grid structures of Earth. These sub-atomic energies serve to allow the acceleration of the awakening of group consciousness for our ascension and the Divine plan of Mother/Father God.

So I asked St. Germain: "What Stargates have we been asked to open?" The Stargates are located along the 1,100 mile Nez Perce trail in Oregon, Idaho, Montana and Wyoming seeded by Chief Joseph in 1877. Historically this path was marked to map Chief Joseph's exodus. In reality it is a living pathway of Light from Earth to Pleiades.

What do these Stargates connect to?

These specific Stargates along the Chief Joseph path are the energy alignment between the constellation Pleiades, also known as the Seven Sisters. These specific points were anchored by Chief Joseph in 1877. The Pleiadian Emissaries of Light hold the vibrational frequency of the fifth to ninth dimensions. Simply put, they can be described as the essence of pure Love, Peace and Harmony. The Pleiadians are teachers and holders of records. Their energy allows us to connect to our Divine Source so we can consciously live as our I AM Presence.

The connection between Pleiades and Nez Perce goes back 10,000 years. It was the Pleiadian Emissaries of Light 10,000 years ago who encoded the DNA of the Nez Perce (People of Peace) with the high vibration consciousness of Peace. I understand the Pleiadians most probably played some part in the fall of Atlantis 12,000 years ago and it was their vow to make amends and assist bringing Mother Earth and humankind back to the Golden Era which was lost.

What is the benefit to mankind to open Stargates?

Stargates allow high vibrational energies to pass through long distances of space, along the space-time continuum. Space-time continuum is the three dimensions of space and the one dimension of time in which physical events are located. Chief Joseph seeded these Stargates to be opened at a future time when the world and humanity were ready to receive this high vibrational activation to assist in the ascension of Mother Gaia and all of humanity.

That time is NOW. I will be intuitively guided to the locations and through the alignment of the crystalline codes I carry in my physical being these long awaited openings will activate. To historians, the trail of the Nez Perce appears to be the exodus of the Nez Perce tribe as they fled from the American settlers and cavalry. In spiritual reality, it was the opportunity for Chief Joseph to seed these Stargates for future activation to assist in our ascension and that of our planet Earth.

My time on the bench was over. I had received my calling and I couldn't pack my bags fast enough, although there was much preparing to do. First, I had to transcribe the channeling with Judith. That being accomplished, there were many unanswered questions and messages I couldn't comprehend. I created a list of questions and scheduled a session to channel with Ahriah. From this channeling I had my "to do" list.

This pilgrimage has been long in the making. Lifetimes actually, but I will speak of only the imminent. To answer this calling I had to be able to hold a certain frequency, much higher than ever before, and be a conduit for Lord Melchizedek and other Ascended Masters to work through me. This process began in November of last year, 2008. My husband Jim and I had taken a trip to Mount Shasta. I had asked for and been granted a visit to Telos by Lord Adama, the High Priest of Telos. Telos is an inner Earth, fifth dimensional Lemurian city located one mile below the surface of Mount Shasta. There are fabulous books written by Aurelia Louise Jones describing the city, its people and culture—a city that will soon be the model for life on the surface of planet Earth when we move into the fifth dimensional consciousness which is upon us.

Jim and I drove to Bunny Flats as far as the late autumn roads and snow would allow us. There we found the trailhead and started hiking. Although it was late November with snow on the ground this day could have been any summer day. A mile down the trail we found a lovely meadow. I spread out my prayer blanket not knowing what to expect or what to do. I was going to lay down with my SETTLEing STONES in hand, meditate and see what happened. I directed Jim to be my guardian, provided him with a journal notebook and pen and instructed him to write whatever inspiration came. Unwittingly, it was his first assignment as Scout. Off we went, side by side our separate ways. Never having done anything like this before I had no idea what to expect. Would I leave my body? Would I be conscious? Would I remember the experience?

A short while later, maybe half an hour I thought, I came out of meditation and prepared to leave—a nice meditation in a nice mountain meadow, nothing more. Jim, on the other hand, had an outpouring of poetry—a book full (which is now self-published). When we reached the car we were both aghast at the time. It had been over three hours, each of us thinking we had been gone an hour. What happened?!

On the ten hour drive back to San Diego I was inspired, guided, and told it was time to cleanse the physical body. The thought and necessity had entered my consciousness to "clean up" many times before, but not the desire. I just wasn't ready. Now the desire was overwhelming. I couldn't wait to start a juice cleanse as soon as I got home even though by normal standards I am an enlightened eater. I honor this temple, my body. I am a consciously healthy person. I follow a vegan diet with moderation. I exercise, I honor holistic practices. This, however, was taking it to the next level.

A few more miles down the road and I was prompted to call my yogi friend Jodi. Last summer she had gone through a body cleanse. Jodi is an "all mental" body so whenever she embarks on anything I can be sure the research is solid and in-depth. I remembered her experience and called. She answered, and if you know Jodi, that is quite a miracle. "Blessed Herbs®," she said. "It's the best!" The name, Blessed Herbs, is all it took for me to know I was being guided! Before we reached home I had ordered the Blessed Herbs internal cleanse and was ready to purify.

The next preparation piece came in the form of the ion cell cleanse, a tool brought to my attention by my visit to Telos. I am sure they have something similar. This is a fifth dimensional technology little understood in the third dimension. To the industry, it is a foot bath that detoxifies the body, helping to eliminate joint pain and other discomforts. On a spiritual level it is nothing short of amazing. The device sends an ionic pulse through the body. In doing so it increases the cellular vibration. Any lower density element is sloughed off. Microscopic images of blood cells before and after have been documented. I actually observed a golden light around each cell after the ion cleanse.

This was the beginning of moving from a carbon based body to a crystalline body structure. Over the next five months through a series of treatments, acupuncture and sessions with different spiritual healers I processed body part by body part, organ by organ, brain, bones, and blood until my body held the crystalline structure we will all have in the new Earth. My DNA strands have slowly increased from 2 to 12 to 18 and after this pilgrimage I hold 21 strand DNA. My physical body was now in attunement with the other three lower bodies—etheric, mental and emotional. I was ready to be downloaded with the necessary frequencies and initiations to take on this calling.

It was time for additional research. Who were the Nez Perce? In their Native language they are the Nimiipuu. I found out the Nez Perce were a prosperous people, a healthy group who stood well over six feet tall when the average height at that time was five feet six inches. Long before women's rights were recognized the Nez Perce respected and revered their women. The Nez Perce women were the owners of the lodges and food sources, freely selling their wares for their own profit. They could choose to leave their husbands without prejudice from their community if they were not treated with honor. Most interestingly, they were allowed intermarriage between other tribes. When this occurred the family and relatives of the spouse became family of the Nez Perce. In this way, all were their brothers' keepers.

The Nez Perce had a love of beauty and aesthetics. They were known for their skilled bead work, often decorating cradle boards, ceremonial garb and their everyday clothing with thousands of ornamental beads and shells. Their handiwork was prized among all nations. They were savvy businessmen, ranchers and ingenious inventors. They bred the finest Appaloosa horses and their stock was sought for its speed and stamina.

The white settlers looked down upon the Nez Perce for being a nomadic group. In reality they were masters of the land and its resources, moving to the warmth and shelter of the canyons in the long, cold winter months, summering in the meadows and following the salmon and buffalo for year round sustenance. The Nez Perce were a people of open minds and open hearts. They embraced the new, allowing people from the outside to share in their land and bounty. Sadly, the American settlers and cavalry did not hold the same values and ideals and in the end took from the Nez Perce what the Nez Perce held to be gifts for all from the Creator. Even though the cultural battle was lost Peace prevailed. Ahead of our time, they lived beyond the illusion of separation in the knowing of Oneness, Peace, Love and Harmony. Their Pleiadian star lineage ran close to the surface. Now, we too, are awakening to this realization.

Probably the most amazing piece of this puzzle and the greatest affirmation came, from all places, the television. One night while Jim was surfing stations he came upon the History Channel and a documentary called *Ancient Astronauts.* It was a show discussing the probability of extraterrestrial life and evidence of it on Earth. Thinking it would interest me he recorded it. A few days later I sat down to watch. Halfway through there was a small blurb on the Pleiades and a graphic outline of the Seven

Sisters constellation. I perked up. Interesting, I thought. Hmm–m, I wonder…

I placed the show on pause, grabbed Jim away from whatever he was doing, searched for a piece of paper and marker and began to trace the outline of the constellation. Jim, shaking his head, wasn't following my line of thinking. Reducing the outline to fit the size of my Stargate map, I overlaid the constellation map onto the seven Stargates I had identified on the Chief Joseph Trail. Jim and I looked at each other in absolute amazement! They matched perfectly. Each of the Seven Sisters stars connected to a Stargate point on Earth. No longer could we think this pilgrimage was something I'd made up for fun. We had just been shown in a very graphic way that this was indeed God work. My intuition and guidance from the Ascended Masters and what could only be found in my heart through Faith and Trust helped me find the way to the Stargates.

The Pleiadian downloading contained two aspects: the first to enhance my sensitivity to geo-magnetic fields. Good thing. In this lifetime I have no compass, no energetic sensitivity. No left, right, up or down. I really need this! Of course, I have Jim, my Scout, but it wouldn't hurt to not rely so heavily and totally on him, and perhaps even once in awhile give him a break on our journey. The second download brought in seven Light packets in the form of Light Rays from the Cosmic Christ through the Pleiadian Councils of Light. These Rays would be projected from my energy body to trigger the activation points in the Stargates when I invoked the sacred tone "Waneen Wan Yan."

There was one more sacred initiation I was asked to undergo—a most sacred honor by Lord Melchizedek. At each Stargate a Melchizedek Merkabah was to be opened. In our Universe there are twelve levels of Melchizedek Merkabah Light Vibration, the highest, God/Source, being twelve. Opening the Stargates required I hold the vibration of at least the 7th level so I could be the bridge from Source at the twelfth level down to the sixth level which is now available on Earth. Even though the planet at this time is not ready for twelfth level Melchizedek energy the Merkabah points in each Stargate must be twelfth level. In order to be this bridge Lord Melchizedek initiated me into the seventh level Merkabah.

The concept of Merkabah is confusing to me. I don't fully understand it but I will do my best to explain. Quoting from the *Keys of Enoch: The Merkabah is a Divine Light vehicle used by the Masters to probe and reach the faithful in many dimensions of the Divine Mind. The Merkabah can take on many forms of brilliant briolette in the physical worlds.*

The Merkabah is a centrifugal light force burning off dross and opening up to accelerated light fields. The Merkabah calibrates kundalini energy which is causing reaction and fire and puts it into its right order—male, female and the God Source energy. It is a way of activating energy and is a form of alchemy, just as one would use a smelter to take out the impurities of gold and leave its purest substance. There is a specific Merkabah for each Stargate, each spinning at a different calibration and different speed bringing in unconditional Love—Divine masculine and feminine. This will become very important at the pivot point Stargate #4, *Heart of the Golden Rose.*

This initiation was most intense. I can only describe it as the feeling a person with bipolar syndrome experiences in a manic episode. I did not sleep for seven days. All of my senses were heightened. I wrote, studied and prepared non-stop with great clarity. Once this new frequency was fully integrated I rested. Then, with the body in order and the job offer accepted, we were ready to embark.

Saturday, May 23, 2009

Jim awoke to the singing of robins—the song to begin our pilgrimage. Little did we know just how important the robins would be throughout our travels! At the time, as I was busily packing, I kept thinking, "Is he going to just sit there and listen to the robins all morning or start helping me?" He was certainly more tuned in that early morning than I was. Guess that's why he's the Scout.

We start our sacred journey where it all began, creating the first circle of infinity, from the Southern California Pacific Ocean to Whitefish Lake Montana. We toss the Pleiadian love stone into the lake. Our prayer is sacred and our guides, The Pleiadian Emissaries of Light, have arrived and are ready for our journey. We bridge the dualities. We merge. We let go of all preparation and succumb to pure Spirit now in the moment. We tone "Waneen Wan Yan," the sacred Pleiadian name given to me 10,000 years ago. This toning vibration will be the "open sesame" for the Stargates for the rest of our pilgrimage as we open the lines to the pure channel of communication to our home in the Pleiades. Chief Joseph, we are ready to have some fun!

And we're off! Getting to Spokane seemed to take longer than I anticipated. By Happy Inn on Highway 2 East en route to Libby I question Jim's directions. The route he selected seemed to have taken us farther north than was necessary. At that moment a bald eagle appeared. When an eagle arrives it has many meanings, but in this case his message was clear: *Detach and rise above the ordinary everyday in order that you may see your life and circumstances with a broader perspective and greater vision.* This was the first of many visits by Chief Joseph simply letting me know there are many paths to the same destination and all are the right path. A valuable lesson learned early on.

Anxious to be officially on our way, we dropped the car off for repairs and transferred everything into the loaner. There were still some car repair worries however, and we hadn't fully disconnected. What was the problem and how much would it cost? Informed that the maintenance warranty we had purchased in San Diego was useless, a $3,000 repair bill was a looming possibility. It would weigh on Jim's mind until Tuesday. I knew God had asked us to embark on this important mission and I also knew this request came with all of the provisions. I've had lots more practice "living on faith." Jim on the other hand is gifted with practicality. "It would be taken care of," I assured him, and so he jokingly remarked to the mechanic, "Hopefully, it's just a few quarts of transmission fluid." And off we went.

The first stop was Confluence Overlook, the place where Donald MacKenzie established a trading post near the Clearwater River. The Nimiipuu were not interested in the fur trade and the trading post never flourished—an historical landmark, not clearly significant to our travels, but a good place to hone our skills of tuning into the geo-magnetic frequency of Mother Earth. I had been gifted with this new talent especially for this journey, but boy, did I need some practice!

We stop at a gully with no water in sight. Given a great deal of imagination it looked like it could have been a confluence a hundred years ago, so we took pictures. We could feel the expansiveness of paradise for hundreds of miles—a taste of what lie ahead. Just a few miles down the road we came across two big rivers "converging." The Confluence! With a big laugh at ourselves we continued on to the town of Joseph, Oregon and our first destination, Wallowa Lake Lodge. It was our plan to spend the entire day, Monday, in Spalding near Lewiston, Idaho where there is much Nez Perce history. As we were passing through however, we were guided to stop at the Nez Perce National Historic Park. It closed at 5:00 P.M. and it was now a little after 4:00 P.M.

The missionary, Reverend Spalding, and his wife were intent on converting the Nez Perce to Christianity. They settled in what we know today as the Washington/Idaho border near Lewiston, Idaho and Clarkston, Washington. It is one of the few areas of Nez Perce country where the hills are open; there is plenty of sunshine, ample river water and fertile farm land. Most of the Nez Perce landscape is high cliffs, steep river gorges and narrow valleys; the hillsides are harsh, sun scorched and waterless, unsuitable for settling.

The Spalding's first order of business was to build a log home and outbuildings—very puzzling to the Nez Perce. Why would a man want to live in a house that could not be moved? To follow the seasons and the animals, people needed to move. The Nez Perce were people of the Wind. They lived in harmony with the land and its bounty, salmon fishing in the spring, harvesting camas root in late summer, hunting buffalo in the fall and wintering in the protective canyons. Eager to please, they cooperated with this strange idea of stationary housing.

The Nez Perce recommended a homestead for Reverend Spalding and his wife near the river, a place called Lapwai, the "Place of the Butterflies." Reverend Spalding, however, preferred another site, a setting which required moving logs many miles. Carrying was women's work, but this job of lugging logs this far was too great; the Nez Perce men, still eager to please, obliged. Reverend Spalding soon discovered his choice home site was too hot with too many biting bugs. He told the Nez Perce he wanted his house moved down river to the spot where they had gathered the logs—the very site the

Nez Perce had first recommended. If the Reverend wanted a house to be moved he should build a light, easily dismantled lodge of poles and skins.

Reluctantly, and less eager to please, they moved his house. If they worked too slowly, they were kicked and whipped. In Nez Perce tradition the "whip man" was hired by parents to correct children's behavior; it was an honored position in the tribe. Adults were never whipped. This was an intolerable insult. Some of the bands adapted to the ways of Reverend Spalding; others were not so sure. Many of his teachings were contrary to their honoring of Mother Earth, their ancestors, and serving the good of their people. It was the trappers who married Nez Perce women who eventually revealed the discrepancies of Reverend Spalding's ways to the Nimiipuu.

The Creator finally spoke through the voice of Earth during the winter of 1845. The snows came early and fell deep. Rivers froze. Food harvested "the Spalding way" was useless. A great hunger came over the land and the medicine men spoke of their forewarning. When the missionaries began speaking more of laws than of Spirit, demanding the Nez Perce give up their ways, the Nez Perce lost faith in such "truth." The greatest insult ultimately occurred during a distribution of goods. The Nez Perce believed a gift was a statement of the person's heart. Chief Joseph was given a tattered and torn blanket in the presence of his people. In disgust he remarked, "I am not a poor man. I have no need of your gifts.

Why do you make fun of me before my own people by giving me a rotten blanket? You put shame on me in the eyes of all the chiefs." With that he withdrew his people from the mission; they returned to their traditional practices, to their freedom, to their Truth.

We were a bit frazzled coming from Spokane, carrying with us like old, unnecessary baggage the energy of the city, car repair challenges and the anxiety of the unknown. Nothing seemed quite right. We were hungry; it had been 10 hours since we had stopped at Starbucks, our only nourishment of the day. Along the way we kept looking for just the right picnic spot and had long ago passed the hunger point. We were hot, too many hours in the car, not sure of how to get where we needed to go.

The Visitors Center was quiet, one lone tourist browsing and the Forest Ranger, Terry, on standby to assist. We watched the video documentary and were reminded of Jim's love for "video tours" going back 18 years, especially in Tijuana and "*The People of the Sun.*" Jimmy and I used to tease him as he dragged us from one boring documentary to another. We laughed and laughed in memory. Some things never change. Terry turned out to be our first helper along the way. He was sweet, soft spoken, knowledgeable and humble. He quietly provided all the information we needed for the next step of our journey. With maps and mementos and a new gift, a wooden flute, we gave our thanks and headed out.

The Visitors Center was part of an expansive historic park including a beautiful picnic site. As we unpacked the cooler for a late lunch/early dinner a robin greeted us. When a robin shows up it is a directive to let go of everything in your life that no longer serves you and to plant seeds for the new. She is telling you to allow as much joy and laughter into your life as you possibly can. She is telling you to sing the song inside of you and share it with the world; follow your spiritual path to your enlightenment, make a wish, be patient and watch it come true. The robin started with us in Whitefish and is here now in Spalding, a sure sign we would come to rely on throughout our travels. Her message: *All is well.* Nourished and replenished we were ready to Journey On.

The Wallowa Lake area is the Nez Perce home. It is the deepest form of the Mother heart energy, the place where they learned the medicine power of the plants, the names and powers of all the animals, and the language of the birds. It is an idyllic place where the Nez Perce held their sacred love for the Divine Feminine Mother. The Mother heart energy was re-gifted to them through the reflection of this lake and the master energies who hold this lake.

When Jim and I arrived Saturday night we were in bliss. It was like taking a step back in time. Our accommodations, once an exclusive hunting lodge only accessible by boat, were built in 1923. That's about all that had changed. We arrived by a curvy two lane road which followed the lake shoreline. Nestled on eight acres and encircled by the soaring peaks of the Eagle Cap Wilderness, we were at the door of a gentle time gone by. Adirondack chairs dotted the expansive grassy stretch to the shoreline, reminiscent of lawn games and leisure. Every sense was sparked by its charm—the sounds of the river, the smell of the pines, the sight of animals, the sunset—all a bit of heaven. Holding hands, gazing into each other's eyes, we couldn't believe we had found such beauty, together, on this journey.

We settled in to our quaint room and made plans for Sunday, our first "real" day on the pilgrimage:

1. Meditate in two big Adirondack chairs overlooking the river adjoining the lake;
2. Find Stargate #1 and open it;
3. Journey back to the town of Joseph to touch the "Big Rocks Lying Around" to receive useful encodings;
4. Go to the gravesite of Old Joseph and render our respect;
5. Get Chai latte;
6. Get band-aids for Jim's finger pricked by a drapery hook (Jim likes to redecorate hotel rooms. It's part of his "nesting");
7. Drive to Minam and pick up something left there hundreds of years ago;
8. Go to Joseph Canyon Viewpoint and find Joseph's Cave, his birthplace;

9. Open Stargate #2;
10. Backtrack and find the four guardian trees, which had caught my attention driving near Asotin the day earlier and where I wished I had stopped;

And finally,

11. Go to Buffalo Eddy, a library of sorts, to receive ancient wisdom from the petroglyphs. Aghhhh!

What were we thinking? Give a former type "A" personality God work to do and she'll "get 'er done!" A bit ambitious! Do you think? After all it was our first official day and we were full steam ahead. Fortunately, this would be the first and the last time we planned our day. We quickly learned this was a God Journey and He was the Master Scout. The pace, the scope, and the ability to make plans and lists or control our destination were out of our hands. A true gift of freedom if only we would let go.

Lesson learned: Surrender to the Will of God. Go with the flow.

Saturday 5/23 4 pm
Nez Perce National Historic Park
Terry O'Halloran the first helper
on the way
sweet, soft spoken, knowing, humble
quietly answered all we needed to know.

We arrived a bit frazzled, coming from
Spokane, city energy, car repair challenge
driving to a place to eat lunch - nothing
seemed just right - one step closer to
Lewiston - kept going past the hunger
point - hot - many hours in the car -
not sure how to get where we need to go -
Arrived and the plan unfolded
The video was an immersion - reminded
me of Jim's love for people of the sun in
Arizona so many years ago.

A beautiful picnic site - robin greeted
us. started the day in WF and here
in Spalding.

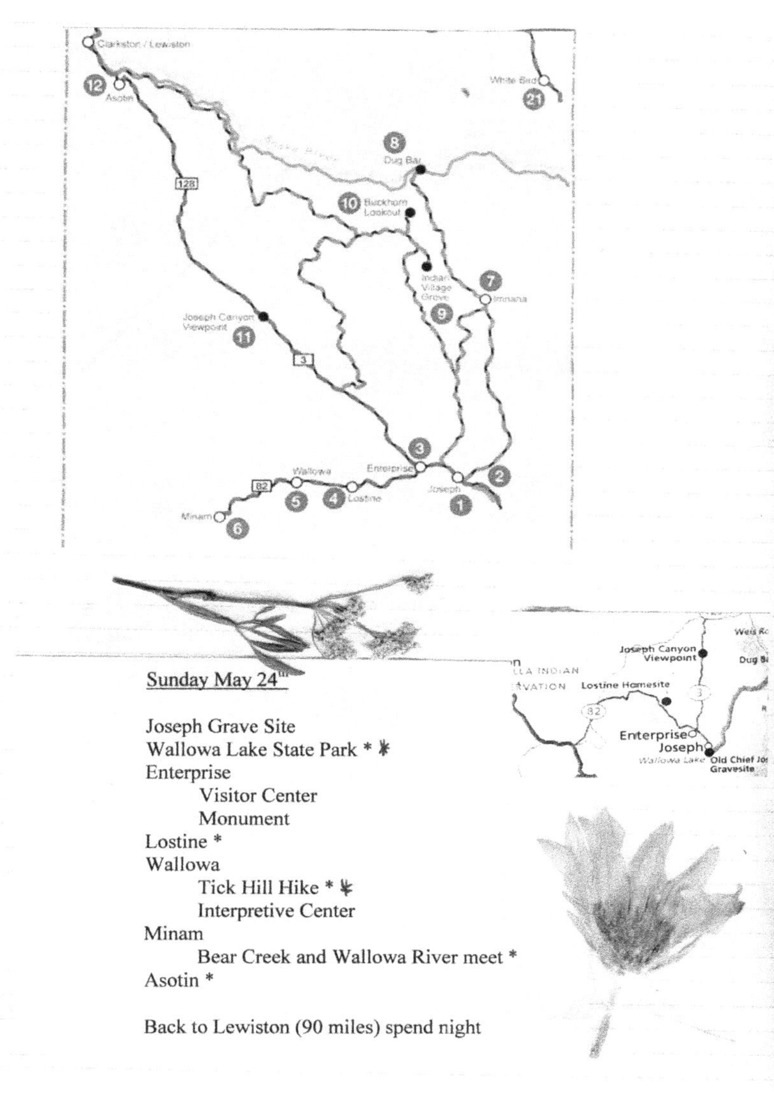

<u>Sunday May 24th</u>

Joseph Grave Site
Wallowa Lake State Park *
Enterprise
    Visitor Center
    Monument
Lostine *
Wallowa
    Tick Hill Hike *
    Interpretive Center
Minam
    Bear Creek and Wallowa River meet *
Asotin *

Back to Lewiston (90 miles) spend night

<u>Saturday, May 23</u>
Whitefish to Spokane – 5 hours
Drop off car and Depart Spokane – ~~3:00~~ 1:11 p.m.
(198 miles to Joseph) Spalding Visitor Center

7:00 p.m. Arrive Joseph Spend the night

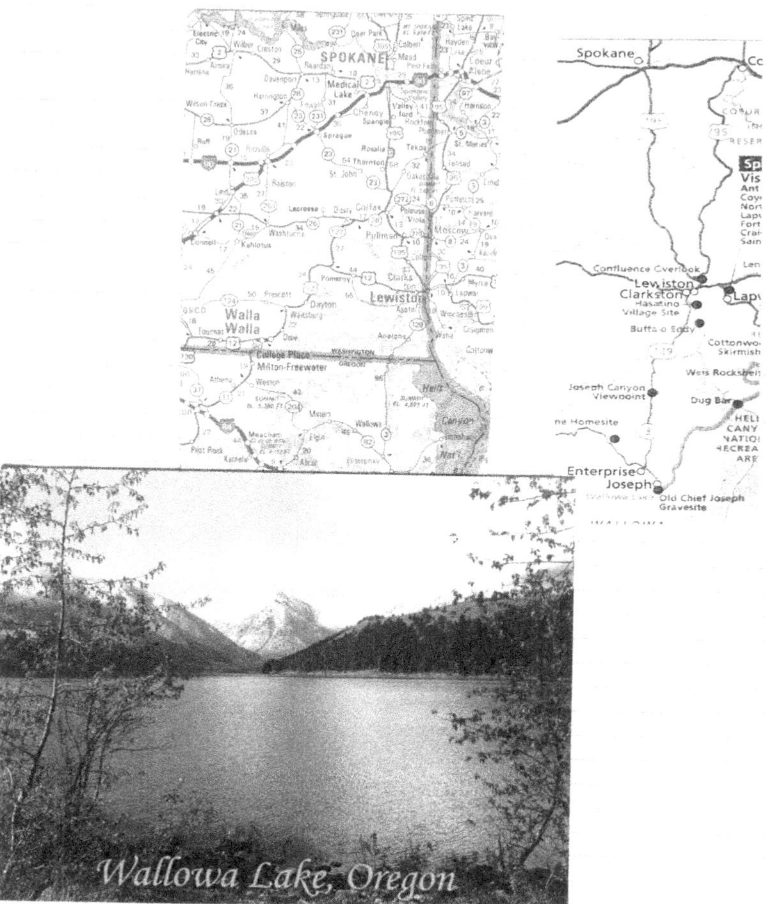

Sunday, May 24, 2009

I was told there is a Goddess of great design who loves me dearly and that I would meet her in the Wallowa Lake area. I would know her by the feeling of Divine Love. I did and I do! The Divine Goddess was working her miracles. Jim's and my love for each other was ascending, just when we thought after thirty-three years we couldn't love each other more. The foretold Goddess was making her presence known. I received the first inkling of her on the third floor of the Lodge outside our hotel room. There was an old picture, an early 1900s print in the style of Maxfield Parrish. It was a portrait of a beautiful woman near a creek bed. Her dress was flowing with the breeze; the sun surrounded her in a halo. It was exquisite, beautiful in an antique way that took my breath away (and confirmation of the message I received weeks earlier that I would meet a Goddess). This message came rushing back. I connected immediately. I wanted the picture as a visible sign of the feeling in my heart. I asked at the front desk if they would sell any of the pictures and I was firmly told, "No, never!" I hadn't expected them to, but I had to ask so it would not remain a nagging regret in my mind. Jim re-created her on the camera and we brought her along. After that I didn't think much of the lady in the dress until we got to Kamiah, Idaho.

After a restful night we took an early morning walk down to where the river merged with the lake. Chief Joseph and a family of eagles, mother, father and babies greeted us. Families of geese and a chorus of birds joined in an early morning symphony. The air was misty; the sky was blanketed in fog, yet rays of sun were making their way through. Unlike the Rockies, the mountains here hold the moisture of the nearby coast. Spring was further along and wildflowers were in bloom. Expanses of green grass were everywhere. It was lush as only landscape can be with the limitless nourishment of water. We prayed and we invoked the blessings of the devas. As I blessed the river flowing into Wallowa Lake with Peace Waters, Jim recalled a road sign he had seen along the way warning people not to put non-native fish and plant species in the waterways. "You are an invasive aquatic species!" We laughed! Yes, and if so, I wear the title proudly. We exchanged waters. Jim was excited: "Let's open the Stargate here!" Intuitively I knew this was not the place. There was too much activity. The river was too loud, too invasive, the tourists too many. Journey On.

We walked along on high alert as to where our first Stargate would be. We assumed it would be lakeside, but as it turned out, we found it on a mountain trail quite a distance away. Nothing had manifested yet. I recalled that each Stargate is aligned with a Sacred Flame or Ray, an Ascended Master,[2] one of the seven physical chakras, a particular tone and an ascension benefit for mankind and Mother Gaia. The twelve Sacred Rays are streams of Divine Energy which emanate from Source. Each Ray expresses and transmits the qualities, characteristics and purpose of the Divine. Simply stated, the Sacred Rays are God virtues. For example, the first Ray is the Divine principle of the Will of God, the second Ray is the Divine principle of Illumination; the third Ray is the Divine principle of Cosmic Love...Each sacred Ray is supported by a Chohan, or Lord of the Ray. This position is typically held by an Ascended Master.

Personally, I love the Spiritual Realm and the Spiritual Hierarchy. It is organization in the highest form—Divine Order. Ironically, it appeals to my many years in the corporate world as an Executive Assistant. The Spiritual Realm is ruled by Law. Promotion is earned purely on works. There is no subjectivity. The Law is the Law. Everyone holds a position based on their ability to hold Light.

---

[2] An Ascended Master is an individual who was at one time embodied here on Earth, just like you and me. After many lifetimes and initiations he gained mastery of this Earth plane, learned all his hard-earned Earth lessons and ascended into his spiritual body. Rather than staying in the higher celestial realms he made the voluntary choice to return to Earth to help mankind achieve its ascension. It is the most selfless gift of Love one can offer.

The requirements for ascension are the mastery of the Sacred Rays. Prior to each incarnation we choose one or two Rays to work with in a particular lifetime. Our life lessons evolve around this mastery. Once we master all of the Sacred Rays we become candidates for ascension. It is at this time that we consciously seek the assistance of an Ascended Master for our ascension process. Upon acceptance by a Master we become that Ascended Master's chela. This is a responsibility of extreme commitment and dedication and a decision of great consequence. The Ascended Master is responsible for the energy he invests in his chela. If we fall short he must make up the energy deficiency. We, in return, become his human vehicle of service on Earth. An Ascended Master must have a physical being to work through. It is an exchange of energy and commitment and must be approved by the Karmic Board. For example, I am a chela of Lord Sananda and Lady Nada. I am guided and directed by the Office of Christ and I work under the sixth Ray of the Love of Christ, selfless service of God and mankind, devotion and spiritual worship. Once we have mastered the Sacred Rays we are considered an enlightened being and we are ready to expand the consciousness of pure God Source through our creativity and service to mankind.

In addition to the Sacred Rays the Stargates are also connected to one of the seven chakras in the physical body, a particular tone which connects us to the sixth dimension and most importantly an Ascension Key, a gift of Divine Love to help in our ascension back to Oneness. The first Stargate, *Dolphin's Halo,* is the blue-green Ray, the color of Earth and other living blue-green planets. It is oversouled by Ascended Master Lord Maitreya. In the Spiritual Hierarchy Lord Maitreya holds the office of the Planetary Christ. This position is typically held for a period of 14,000 years (2,000 years to bring in and master each of the seven Rays) before the Planetary Christ moves on to another position and a new Master assumes the responsibilities of Planetary Christ. Lord Maitreya has held this position for a little over 2,000 years. In his position he is currently greatly assisted by Lord Sananda, the name of Jesus in the higher realms. Jesus was oversouled by Lord Maitreya and during his lifetime Lord Maitreya was Jesus' Spiritual "Father." He was the sponsor of his noble mission. Like all of us, Jesus was no different. We must each have an Ascended Master to mentor and sponsor our ascension.

This first Stargate was seeded to open the Will of God; it is connected to the throat chakra. It is the consummation of Will coming into the voice of "Yes." It is closely affiliated with the devic realm, the realm of elementals, fairies and devas. It was important to open this Stargate in the beginning to receive the support of the devas for the rest of our pilgrimage. Some of the Stargates are guarded by the devas and unless they receive the devic symbol they will not let anyone close to that Stargate to work the energies. The devic symbol is the tone "Wan," the first syllable of Waneen Wan Yan. They will feel this vibration and will work with us.

We found our way to Wallowa Lake Trailhead. This is the land where Chief Joseph grew up as a child. Here he said, "I love this land more than all the rest of the world." We can see why. There were a number of trailheads to choose from and naturally we chose the Chief Joseph Trail. Heading off to the right we walked up a slight slope to a fork. There we took the fork to the right identified by trail marker #1803 *Chief Joseph Trail.* As we followed Wallowa Creek we came to a bridge. The view of the Wallowa Mountain peaks was awe inspiring and we stopped to take pictures. They reminded us of the mountain range of Mount Shasta, majestic, snow covered, granite peaks reaching for the sky. We had received many gifts on that beautiful trip in November. Looking back, I now understand how our trip to Mount Shasta (another story in itself) was preparation for this journey, the actual beginning. We were drawn to one peak in particular, Mount Aneroid. Jim stopped to take pictures and clicked away, but as he reviewed the pictures, there was no sign of the mountain peak on film, merely a cloudy glow. Mystified, he kept clicking. Still no image—the first inkling that this journey was not of the third dimension world—verification that nothing we would encounter would surprise us on this Divine assignment.

Later, at a small boutique in the town of Joseph, Jim found a photo of the mountain range which included Mount Aneroid. As he was paying the cashier, he shared his story. She looked at him with an amused expression and a wry smile. "Aha," is all she said—a knowing, humoring acknowledgement without further explanation, unable or unwilling to reveal the hidden mountain's secret.

We were told there are etheric masters who reside in the mountains and they decide whether the visions will be held or not. Because the people of Mother Earth have not fully evolved to a fifth dimensional consciousness of Love and Peace, there is still chance their appearance could be misused and they could be at risk of harm. They camouflage their form energy for their own protection and for the protection of less evolved souls so they will not incur the karma should this knowledge be misused. There is no need for us to be concerned. We discovered this to be something that will happen again and again. As we traveled on and became more attuned to the higher frequencies we noted the veils became thinner and we were gifted with sightings, messages, and languages too Divine to behold. We knew we would receive visions, or not, for reasons we may not be aware of, knowing it is all in Divine Order.[3]

By now you are probably wondering where these messages come from? How do I learn these things? Who are my "guides" and the Ascended Masters of whom I speak? I will digress and explain.

---

[3] Some day we will all be able to live in harmony, in or out of form, on the surface of Earth or within, and we will all be present and visible to each other. Until then we can only imagine.

I work with a soul team—friends on Earth who help me connect with my formless friends. One of my most Divine friends is Judith, who is a trance medium and channel. Judith has a Divine connection to Source bridging the gap between the formless and manifest form. She has dedicated her life to being of service to the awakening of Heaven on Earth. Judith receives her information from the 13:13:13 which is the perfect geometric code for the Office of the Christ collaborating with the Mind of God for the higher frequencies of ascension. I don't pretend to understand this, but I know what she brings forth is pure God Essence and of the highest Truth. That's all I need to know and I am forever grateful that I have such a friend in Judith to bring my work forward.

The 13:13:13 is a geometric portal of the Office of Christ moving into synergy of Mind of God and opening the vortex for the download of Wisdom. This is where Judith is receiving her information and why it is so accurate. Judith is an amazing conduit in terms of her clarity and her surrendering to the release of new information. Like *Mission: Impossible* she brings forth "job opportunities" for me to accept or not accept as I choose. It was Judith who brought forth the Ascension Keys, among other things. There is a synergy between us and a partnership, a contract we agreed to long before we incarnated in this lifetime. Sometimes I get glimpses of our past life relationships and it is like reuniting with the most sacred friend. Judith presents the information for a "job" to be done and it is my work to carry it forward. What she gives me I give back to her in affirmations, consolidation and the fruits of her labor. I will always have Ascended Master teachers in and out of body, but Judith is very adept. She has a contract with me given directly from the Ascended Masters to assist me in my calling. Without Judith I would still be bumbling around and searching for my "purpose."

One day while visiting Judith I requested a channeling session. I was ready for my next mission. I had been holding a high vibrational Light frequency since bringing forth the Ascension Keys. It doesn't sound like much, but trying to stay in a state of grace at my level of Light was a test! From outward appearances, I wasn't doing much of anything—meditating, gardening, walking on the beach, time in the loft, a sublime life to be sure, but I was ready to take on a new project. "Let's channel" I requested. And in came Chief Joseph. Twenty-five days later Jim and I find our selves on the pilgrimage of our lives opening our first Stargate, *Dolphin's Halo,* thousands of miles away from San Diego.

As I mentioned, I don't pretend to understand any of this on a conscious level, but energetically I know it is my Truth. So when my mind needs to be satisfied and I seek understanding, I turn to another member of my soul team, Ahriah. I take the information I receive from Judith, put it into a question/answer format then ask for a meeting with the Ascended Masters through Ahriah who can best explain in English what I have been told. Ahriah, too, is a channel of the highest caliber—my spiritual communicator and conduit. Instead of learning on my own, I have found that I can work with Ahriah like *CliffsNotes* and get the answers I need to proceed in half the time. We worked well this way when I was inspired to develop the SETTLEing STONES®, Peace Waters™ and other God products. It was like having a board meeting and marketing session with the Ascended Masters. I highly recommend it!

Ahriah works entirely differently than Judith. Judith connects to a stream of consciousness and flows. Ahriah works in a question/answer format whereby the highest source of wisdom comes through to answer my specific questions. It is a partnership made in heaven to be sure. I am able to receive encodements and initiations through Ahriah. The Masters have allowed Ahriah to be my channel for this purpose because they will erase whatever is in her state of consciousness that is intended only for me to receive in that specific moment. She is not receiving the encodements and initiations. Rather, she is fluidly moving the information through her vocal cords and into the vortexes into my body as is necessary for me to retain. Ahriah does not remember what we are doing and the Masters tell me this is as it should be. Back and forth we go, Judith, me, Ahriah. In this way the ultimate Divine plan of opening the Stargates, seeded 10,000 years ago by the Pleiadians then marked by Chief Joseph in 1877 unfolded for me in order to take the next step of activation.

After the baffling encounter with Mount Aneroid we continued. Crossing the raging creek Jim was nudged by a rock outcropping. I had been following heart-shaped stones along the pathway like the story of Hansel and Gretel looking for the spot. Slowly, we were releasing the habits and entrainment we rely upon in our everyday third dimension world; we were beginning to listen to our environment and be open to the signals and signs given to us by the elementals, the plant, mineral and animal kingdoms. We were discovering what it truly means to be guided.

The rock outcropping at first looked like an eagle. Jim noticed his black eye, then his beak and forehead. As he gazed, it morphed into a dolphin or a whale. We learned later that many people are drawn to this rock and most people see a turtle. Thus it is named Turtle Rock. Jim knew it was the entrance, the key to entering the Stargate. There was no need to doubt. Jim was the Scout and he was perfect in this position. He's relied on his intuition many times; it had served him well in his teens and early adult years, affording him protection. He had not lost this Divine gift. Me, on the other hand, I'm still learning to read signs, symbols and follow my intuition. I am challenged by left, right, north, south—the simple every day third dimension directions we rely on.

Upon turning the corner after passing Turtle Rock I could feel the energy shift. I can only describe it as womb-like. We were surrounded by mountains. The roar of the river had lessened, the peacefulness was evident. The air was still. We felt we were close. As we traveled on our journey "feeling" would become "knowing" but on this first exploration we had not fully accepted our intuitive wisdom. Until *Swallows Window,* the third Stargate, we would still be hampered by doubt. Thereafter, there was no place for error.

On a little bluff by some fallen trees we noticed a pile of rocks to the right of the trail. The stones were all black except one of pure white quartz. This is a symbol, a sign I did know. The white quartz rocks have been my mineral guide since my awakening to my I AM Presence—the Pleiadian love stones from the beach and the Illuminate from Crystal Hill in the desert had keyed me into the messages from the mineral kingdom. There was no mistaking this was the Stargate. A few yards further we came upon a perfectly round grassy meadow with mountain peaks visible to the south. One large sparkling, granite rock, larger than a basketball marked the spot, the only rock in the grassy meadow. It had recently been moved and there was a depression where it originally laid. We were guided to dig and bury the sacred bundle in the impression then place the rock back in its original resting place. Sacred Union!

The sacred bundles were inspired long before I knew their purpose. I love rocks, feathers, pieces of wood; sea shells and sea glass. I am a collector, a rock hound and over the years I have accumulated jars and boxes of unique gifts of Mother Earth (before I knew better to take pictures and leave only footprints). When I was asked to make this Stargate pilgrimage I knew something special should be left ceremoniously at each stopping place. I had no idea how many Stargates there would be so I prepared for twenty. Thank you God there were only seven, plus the two anchor points in Whitefish and San Diego for a total of nine, or we'd still be on the trail!

In my professional life I was a great marketer, brander, and packager. Aesthetics were always paramount, often more important than the content for me. I understand the power of appeal through visual sensation—I can take the simplest article and turn it into a beautiful work of art. My eye for marketing served me well in those days and now it is an incredible gift for the Peace Waters products. So naturally, creating sacred bundles was joyous for me. I had all the ingredients; it was just a matter of assembling. I used the same handmade batik pouches I use for the SETTLEing STONES and in each batik pouch I placed the following:

Three Pleiadian Love Stones

These are small, smooth, ocean tumbled quartz stones found along the Southern California coast between Winter Solstice and Spring Equinox. They hold the high vibration Light energy from the Pleiadian realm. The stones connect us to the frequencies of unconditional Love and Peace. I make Shima Peace Pendants from these stones and anyone who wears the pendants is touched by their essence. They become walking Emissaries of Light increasing and spreading the Light vibration on Earth. I felt they would do the same for the Stargates so I gathered enough to put three in each pouch.

Rose Quartz and Clear Quartz

Rose quartz is all about Love and emotional healing. It is the supreme stone of Love and I include it in everything I do so of course it would be part of the bundle. Rose quartz carries the loving consciousness of the Christ and other heart-centered Ascended Masters. It is one of the most powerful of the spiritual mineral kingdom. I also include clear quartz which serves as an amplifier. I find it never hurts to turn up the amps when we're working with Light and Love!

Illuminite

I placed a piece of white quartz that I call Illuminite in each pouch. I discovered Illuminite over a year ago on a sacred Crystal Hill camouflaged by the immensity and monotony of the Mojave Desert. Unless directed to this sacred spot it remains anonymous—little did I know then its true purpose. The Pleiadians, along with other pure Light Beings of the galactic plane, use Illuminite as a beacon to descend and anchor high frequency Light vibration energy to assist in our evolution and ascension. How perfect for the Stargates. It serves as a radio transceiver, a lighthouse for the Galactic Emissaries of Light to easily locate us through the veils of physicality. Illuminite helps raise our vibration opening to Peace, Love and Harmony. It also protects us from lower frequencies by merging these energies back with her God Self and ascending to the fifth dimension and beyond—exactly what we are being asked to do on this pilgrimage.

Dove Feather

At our home in San Diego Jim has created a wild bird aviary of sorts near the front entrance. We live in a small duplex in the suburbs of San Diego so the gathering of so many birds is quite unusual in this urban setting. We are greeted each day by quail, doves, finches, hummingbirds, ravens and an assortment of other birds we have not yet identified. There is a pecking order. Each bird comes at its allotted time and they enjoy the seed and birdbath on their schedule. Only the hummingbirds get a bit territorial. The little guys! This practice of ours is disturbing to our neighbors for as Jim feeds them daily with gourmet seed, the neighbors can only see the possibility of attracting rats. The rats know, however, that this is not for them and for the last five years they have not come near. Only the HOA security monitor and the occasional notice to "cease and desist" mar the Peace of this bird sanctuary. As a gift for Jim's outpouring of Love the birds leave an occasional feather. We collect them with joy and they grace our house along with rocks, shells and other genuine finds. So naturally a dove feather, the symbol of Peace, would be part of our bundle. After all, Chief Joseph is the purest expression of Peace.

The Ascension Keys

Each Ascension Key is a symbol in Light Language holding a Divine frequency. There are many, many Divine Principles. I have chosen 15 to bring into print: Oneness, Love, Wisdom, Discernment, Grace, Forgiveness, Majesty, Divinity, Truth,

Authorship, Patience, Manifestation, Gratitude, Sacred Resonance, and Peace. These symbols were channeled to me through Judith and then drawn in their geometric perfection by our son Jimmy. I created a book and cards bringing the spiritual art form into a tool for prayer and contemplation. I have since made these beautiful symbols into one inch squares, placed them in a satin pouch and included them in the Stargate bundles to bless the land with these Divine God Virtues wherever they may go.

So you can see how all of the *Peace Waters* creations and manifestation have led up to the tools for this sacred Pilgrimage. But I'm not done yet.

Elohim Peace Waters

The Elohim Peace Waters is most important to the opening of the Stargates. These sacred waters are collected from an identified portal in Whitefish, Montana. They carry the current of the Divine Principle, Peace. Through a ceremonial process I place the waters, the Pleiadian Love Stones and enhydro smoky quartz from Lolo, Montana into a quartz crystal singing bowl toned to the heart chakra and the musical note "F." Once assembled, I infuse and energize this sacred water with unconditional Love and bottle it for sharing. By dispersing the Elohim Peace Waters in the waterways near your home or in your bath you emanate the pure Peace vibration throughout the world, in essence becoming a channel of Peace and Love. In return you receive the most beautiful gift of all: the benefits of Grace, Love, Divinity, Hope, Wisdom and Celebration—ultimate Peace in your life. Naturally, the water couldn't be put in the bundle so we poured the waters into each Stargate site along with holy water from Lourdes given to me by my friend Bill.

Santuario de Chimayo Sacred Soil

Lastly, we included sacred soil from Chimayo, New Mexico. In approximately 1810 a Chimayo Friar saw light bursting from the hillside. Following the light he began digging on the hillside and found a crucifix. He named the crucifix Our Lord of Esquipulas. Three times it was removed from this site and brought to Santa Cruz. Each time it mysteriously disappeared and was found back in its hole on the hillside. A chapel was erected and miraculous healings followed. It became known as the "Lourdes of America." Soon after the chapel was built on this site, a sacred sand pit called El Posito opened behind the altar. Even more miraculous healings manifest at El Posito and over 300,000 people come to this healing sand every year. Judith moved to Chimayo in 1990 where she has experienced the miracle of Chimayo Valley in her own personal healing. Before our departure Judith gave me some of the sacred Chimayo soil from El Posito, additionally blessed by a gentleman who channels Archangel Gabriel. I guess you could say it is extra blessed!

After opening *Dolphin's Halo* we were in a state of Divine awe. The symbols and directives guiding us and the nudges by nature, animals and rocks taking us to the exact location were amazing. But we soon discovered that opening some of the other Stargates would not be so easy. We walked back down the trail and treated ourselves to a picnic lunch, then off to our next destination: "Big Rocks Lying Around."

There's an area of land near the town of Joseph known as "Big Rocks Lying Around." It is exactly what its name implies—big rocks lying around—huge boulders called moraine, left from glacier runoff millions of years ago. I was told "These rocks are stone people, stone beings, and when you find this place you are to make personal contact with the rocks. Go around and touch as many of them as you can and you will receive encodements. In return you are to make a tobacco offering to the stone people as thanks for the unseen gifts you received from them." Okay, whatever!

The remains of elder Chief Joseph, Joseph's father, were reburied in this memorial gravesite in 1926 after the original resting place had been vandalized one too many times. It's a typical graveyard. Nearby other graves of the Nez Perce and settlers are scattered about. For unexplained reasons, old gravesites interest Jim so he was excited to make this stop. As for me, I just wanted to stop and go.

The cemetery was peppered with brightly colored flowers and ornaments. It was Memorial Day weekend, the perfect time to visit a cemetery all dressed up for the holiday. As we approached the monument Jim pointed out that this was most likely a diversion, a decoy to draw tourists while protecting the real site. I love his scouting instincts! We walked around, heading away from the tourist signs and found a place off to the side of the park holding a peaceful glow. Here we gave our thanks and prayers to elder Chief Joseph.

Next we headed into town for gas, to wash all the bugs off the windshield, and get first aid for Jim's pierced finger. The bugs on the windshield intrigued Jim to the end of the journey. Perhaps there's a message even in this! It's hot. The dewy, cool, misty foggy morning is only a memory. We're dirty and dusty, a bit cramped in the car, and dog-tired. Nevertheless, with a full tank and a clean windshield we Journey On toward Minam.

Minam could hardly be called a town, but it is on the map. A pull out, actually, with a boat launch and a restroom. A place only river rafters and fisherman would find appealing. A place, I was told, where something was left. Perhaps one of the medicine people or sacred Elders died or left something important to be released. That's our mission. There is an energy we are to receive that will be helpful on our pilgrimage.

Before we open the Stargates we must have the blessings of the Ancestors. Stop by stop we are receiving each blessing necessary before we can carry on to the next step. With Jim's guidance and love of structure we managed to stay on the path and avoid the shortcuts I kept finding all too inviting. First at *Dolphin's Halo* from the devas, then the encodements for "Big Rocks Lying Around" and now at Minam we receive blessings from the Ancestors. Once we have traveled through the Ancestors see our goodness and they bless us. Minam was way off the path to the west. I guess the higher realms like a good laugh as much as anyone; they probably just want to see how committed we are and what we'll do no matter what is asked. I don't share this thought with Jim. While I find the Ascended Masters and other etheric beings have quite a sense of humor, he wouldn't find it funny. Perhaps this diversion was for their amusement. Who knows?

We bumbled around trying to figure out where we should be and ended up at a boat launch where the Bear Creek and Wallowa rivers meet. It didn't look like much. We tried to imagine how it looked hundreds of years ago before the parking lot and pit toilet. When I can't get a feeling of where we are supposed to BE, I turn to my pendulum. It seems to give me some direction, like those skilled in map reading and the use of a compass as their valuable directional tool. I find my way by using the pendulum—"Yes" or "No" points me in the right direction. By the end of our journey this wouldn't be necessary. Somewhere along the way I found my inner knowing and learned to Trust. Gift Given!

At the confluence of the rivers we gave gifts of sacred leaf tobacco and cornmeal to return the abundance to this land and its people. We blessed it with the sacred Chimayo soil in order to bring all land and Earth and its kingdoms into Oneness. And finally, we blessed the waterways with Peace Waters and received waters in return for blessings in the future. We asked the Ancestors for their blessings on our way. Gift Given, Gift Received. This completed our prayer ceremony. Off to Stargate #2.

"We have big work to do" I said absentmindedly thinking of the enormity of our pilgrimage. Jim stopped me. "It's not work. It's your passion. From now on it's your 'calling.'" I like that. "Okay." I agree, even though sometimes it does feel like work. It will take some time for me to fully integrate and transmute what I know as "work" to a "calling." After all I've been "working" all my life, but that's okay since Jim has lots of time to remind me as we Journey On.

Let me tell you about Jim as I see him through my eyes and feel him through my heart. Jim is a handsome man, 56 years old, 6 feet tall, physically fit. He has a full head of blonde curly hair which he delights in me "styling" each morning. And by that I mean a few runs through with my fingers. He has the same whimsical childish smile and sense of adventure as when I met him 33 years ago at the age of 23. You may remember in the early 2000s in Southern California when the term "metro-sexual" was coined. It described a masculine man who was in touch with his feminine self and comfortable with it. Metrosexual types have impeccable taste and enjoy the finer things in life. They take pride and care in their personal appearance and aren't afraid to get facials, manicures and massages. They enjoy taking care of their body and their spirit as we goddesses do—simple acts of self-love we have delighted in forever. Jim typifies the metro-sexual stereotype—a masculine persona with a warm heart.

Jim's main recreation, hobby, and sport are me. I am all consuming, but he also enjoys his workouts combining Pilates with weight lifting finessed by a wiry little trainer, Beth, who is motivated to see just how far she can push this middle-aged man. Beth's efforts have resulted in the body of a 38-year-old in a 56-year-old's frame. Jim has a love and passion for cooking, one of his many creative outlets. He is a master chef having cooked at the finest restaurants in America, including one rated among the top 25 in the world. He has cooked at the James Beard House, the Vatican of chef de cuisine. He expresses his love through his cooking. I laugh when I remember the time in our relationship when my love for Jim was measured by my appetite for his meals. If I ate a lot, I really loved him. If I wasn't hungry on a given day, then my love for him had diminished. Thankfully, I am not physically as big as my love for him and his food, but the combination of food and love has its challenges!

Jim is eager to please. We both carry that trait, sometimes to a fault evidenced by a funny story about hearts of palm. For years we put hearts of palm in our salads, me thinking Jim savored them; he thinking I liked them. Neither one of us cared for them, but to please the other it was always a part of our salads. One day as we were each picking around them we discovered that neither of us had a taste for hearts of palm. That's the way Jim is. He is selfless and generous to the point of giving all he has if he thought you needed or wanted it, or eat hearts of palm in spite of his distaste. He'll hold nothing for himself if there is someone else in need. My mother used to say (actually her only complaint about him ever): "The problem with Jim—he's too generous. He needs to learn not to be!" That describes Jim.

His greatest creative expressions are writing poetry and photography, but he also enjoys the adventure of the unknown so whether he's familiar with it or not, he's not afraid to go at it with his heart and soul. Take this pilgrimage of opening Stargates, for example. It's not his passion or his calling, but he's right there, ready to be the Scout. He has proven to be more adventurous and more in tune than me. I do my part, but Jim actually takes us on the route God has planned for us. He enjoys all sports especially attending live pro sports events. When our son Jimmy was growing up, he was at every game, first coaching him on his way to a pro baseball career (Dad's dream, not Jimmy's) and these days as a PGA Professional Golf Pro. Golf was the one sport Jim didn't take to, but out of love for our son he learned to play. Not very well and not with a lot of enjoyment, but he learned nonetheless so he could talk the talk and be part of Jimmy's pro career.

One of Jim's greatest desires is to be a grandfather. Having only one child, he has way too much love and *joie de vivre* to share. At this writing we are blessed with the announcement we will be grandparents. This, along with all of his desires, will come to fruition. Jim has always lived with an open heart and will reap the benefits of his beautiful soul as the promise of the Golden Era emerges. He works tirelessly in his business as a commercial property manager of retail shopping centers. He's a one man show with a big job—finding solutions to problems. He is a gifted mediator and had his past not been peppered with the malfeasances we all committed in our youth in the 70s he would be a most valued public servant, an ambassador to the world in the name of Peace and Harmony. Jim's heart sings a different tune these days; his passion is not with his business as in earlier years, but he does it with the same fervor and dedication as if it were his greatest joy. For now it's a completion of his karma, his way of chopping wood and carrying water. As the promises of the future near I know in my heart he will be able to express himself in the pure God essence of what I have come to enjoy with his support.

Jim can best be classified as a "sport." He'll try anything from jumping off a 60 foot cliff into the Flathead River to going on a Stargate adventure with the woman he loves. Jim is funny; he can entertain a crowd for hours. He's a stand up comedian—my personal show. He is an anomaly, a child his parents couldn't understand, tried to figure out, and ultimately quit trying out of frustration. The adventurer and explorer left home for Europe when he was 16 and used his college funds to buy a bar and grill in Portugal—a free spirit indeed. He chose, or rather God chose us for each other. Our relationship hasn't come without sacrifice, but a price we willingly pay for our priceless Love. Anyone who comes into contact with Jim—friends, acquaintances, male or female—immediately takes an intense liking to him. His childish good looks, his sense of humor, his ability to laugh spontaneously and always remain lighthearted makes people want Jim around or for their own and believe me, many women have tried using all their guiles and wiles. And yet he has steadfastly stood with me. Our love is beyond human concept—two souls hand picked by God to be together.

Jim is comfortable in his own skin and thereby makes everyone around him comfortable. He is a true master. For the many years I have been on my spiritual journey, seeking, seeking, seeking to find God outside of myself he would watch patiently wondering when I would look inside to find and see "me." I was always trying to bring him along, to see the Light, to become enlightened. Little did I realize he already was an enlightened being—there is no seeking for him, he already holds God in his heart. It just is; there's nothing to think about or do; there's no spiritual path to follow. He is it. That's Jim. A man's man, a boy's boy, the perfect expression of the balance of the feminine and masculine, not afraid of being who he is, not afraid of showing emotion or expressing Love. Not afraid to be the Ruby Knight, the strong warrior and protector, and now, the Scout. He jokes that the reason we've been married for over 30 years is because every year I change my hair, my clothes, my style, my personality. He likes being married to a new woman each year. I can't say the same. Jim is the steady one, stalwart, the responsible one, the one who loves against all odds. I love him deeply and so it is.

By now we're tired, meaning I'm tired. Jim, he's the energizer bunny and just keeps on going. It is early evening and we've put lots of miles on the road. It seems like days since we were in the rich lushness of Wallowa Lake. And it was only this morning! We've only opened one Stargate. I am beginning to feel all the stops that aren't Stargates—Minam, Elder Joseph's gravesite, Big Rocks Lying Around—are superfluous, but Jim, in his ever patient, never tiring way reminds me we can't get to the next Stargate until we open all the keys leading up to it. I agree. I am just tired. I'm used to my daily stone and crystal naps!

In retrospect, little did we know this really was just the beginning; that our journey would take us 4,349 road miles in eight days (not including air miles from Las Vegas to Kalispell); little did we know there would be too many miracles to count and too many moments of laughter and surges of love to remember. At this moment however, there is no time, no miles and the sweet essence of God keeps us moving.

We arrive at Joseph Canyon Viewpoint, a typical tourist pull out along the highway. There's a steady stream of vehicles with people popping in and out clicking photos of the immense overlook. It is breathtaking and enormous. Having never been to the Grand Canyon I can only imagine miles and miles of canyon—the immensity is overwhelming. This particular canyon is the overlook of one of the winter homes of the Nez Perce. The American settlers misguidedly judged the Nez Perce as nomadic, without roots. In reality they were experts at embracing the gifts of Mother Earth; they simply knew this was a place of warmth and protection in the cold winter months. It was here that Joseph was born in a cave along the east bank of the creek in 1840.

Stargate #2 is a seven-pointed star oversouled by Ascended Master Metatron.[4] Lord Metatron carries the Divine blueprint of the Immaculate Concept. The Immaculate Concept is the pure perfection of God Source undistorted by human, galactic or other miscreation and misconception. It is pure God Essence. Mother Mary held the Immaculate Concept for Jesus so he could complete his discipleship. She had to have the singular focus to be able to draw forth a Divine thought form and then be able to hold it. Before birth we are able to see the Immaculate Concept clearly on the cosmic screen, but once embodied, the bands of forgetfulness surround us and our vision becomes clouded. We must be so

---

[4] Lord Metatron is the guardian of the threshold between form and non-form. He opens the gates of consciousness to our own divinity. Metatron is the beginning and the end, the Alpha and the Omega. Like a prism, Metatron divides the white Light into different colors and the energy of Unity emanating from Source into separate parts, giving each of us a glimpse of our piece of the puzzle when we are ready to receive our Divine blueprint. He helps in the intensification of vibrations. As we move through our ascension process more and more of the templates necessary to carry this higher Light are encoded by Lord Metatron into our physical and Light bodies. He is one of our most important companions on our path of ascension.

strong in our desire for God and our dependence on Faith to not allow any force within us or without us to destroy that image. The Immaculate Concept is Perfection. The Sacred Ray of the second Stargate is magenta. The Magenta Ray is the ninth solar aspect of Deity and its Divine qualities are harmony, balance, assurance and confidence. This Stargate aligns with the root chakra. The activation tone is "Wa" the first syllable of the name Waneen.

As we're getting our gear together to head out to find the Stargate we're stopped by a man eager to engage in conversation. At this point I am open to all because who knows who the next helper will be along the way (I had yet to encounter what lay ahead in Kamiah in the form of saboteurs) so I eagerly welcomed him. Jim, Mr. Gregarious, was not his usual self and stood off to the side. The man began by inquiring about mountain peaks. Even though I was completely unfamiliar with this area, like an expert, I pulled out the photo Jim purchased of the Wallowa Mountains. Still, Jim did not engage. The man was not really interested in mountain peaks; I guess it was a conversation opener. His real interest was the woeful state of world affairs. He delved into real estate, the recession, and every other malady being reported in the present day's news. Whoa! How quickly we drop into the third dimension. This doesn't feel good and it surely has nothing to do with the God reality in which we've been immersed. I stop, rather abruptly. Enough of this and with a curt "Gotta go!" we move on. Very strange—had I known then what I know now I would have handled this very differently. I had a big lesson waiting for me ahead, a funny encounter, a missed signpost, an overlooked warning by my guides.

We start walking, looking for a sign to the Stargate. There are no paths so we are scouring the hillside. It is steep, rocky, and difficult to maneuver. One misstep will hurtle us down the canyon; Jim's on high alert watching every step I take. To the right of us is the highway, the sound of cars and the steep terrain are not the ideal place we were expecting. Now Jim is tired. He never admits it, but I can tell. He's ready to stop anywhere. And since he's the Scout he has the authority to say, "Here's the spot" (except that after 33 years I still hold veto power). I keep saying, "No, not here." We slip and slide and stumble and finally decide this isn't working and cross the highway. Easier trekking for sure, but there are still lots of holes and rocks to twist ankles so the going is slow. I bring out my trusty pendulum. It doesn't move. It stays dead still. "Thanks a lot," I'm thinking, "Where are you when I need you?"

We come upon a meadow rounded by pine trees. In the center we are both drawn to a huge Ponderosa Pine. The tree is ancient—majestic, regal, patriarchic. It appears it's no longer alive but it still stands towering over 300 feet. Most interesting is the beautiful iridescent green moss making its home on all its stately branches—death giving home to life; life giving beauty to the ancient. THIS WAS IT. We settled in and opened the Stargate with ceremony.

The ceremony evolved simply and smoothly. We hadn't planned for it to be that way. This was under Divine Guidance and each piece was brought to us by friends and Light Workers, all sharing in the opening of the Stargates. I weaved a few of my favorite prayers together for the invocation from the inspirational words of the Ascended Masters Teaching Foundation, The New Age Study for Humanity's Purpose and others who I give credit to but can't remember their source.

Beloved I AM Presence, Father/Mother God, Lord Jesus Christ, Divine Holy Spirit, Holy Mother Mary, Krishna, Babaji and Yogananda; Chohans of the Seven Rays—Maha Chohan, El Morya, Kuthumi, Paul the Venetian, Serapis Bay, Hilarion, Lady Nada and St. Germain; Archangels—Michael, Raphael, Gabriel, Zadkiel, Uriel, Jophiel and Chamuel, Haniel, Tzafkiel, Metatron and Melchizedek; Peace Elohim, Mahatma, Lord Maitreya, Sanat Kumara, Helios, Vesta, Djwal Kul, Vyamus and all Emissaries of Light who have come to assist Jim and Shima on this sacred pilgrimage of Peace as we fulfill our part of God's glorious Divine Plan to open and activate the Stargates located along the pathway of Chief Joseph.

Beloved I AM Presence, St. Germain, Archangel Zadkiel and Holy Amethyst: Blaze in, through, and around Jim, Shima and this sacred land the transmuting Violet Flame thy sacred fire. Purify and transmute all energies ever miscreated by us in all time, space and dimension, knowingly or unknowing. Keep this flame sustained and powerfully active.

Beloved I AM Presence and Beloved Archangel Michael: Intensify your pillar of pure Light substance in, through, and around Jim and Shima, charged with your invincible protection, all powerful and almighty.

Beloved I AM Presence and Beloved Goddess Energy of Mother Gaia; we connect with the elementals, the four directions, the devas and every level of co-creation between dimensions. We honor you and are blessed to be One with you with the Divine Mind and the Heart of the Mother Goddess. We ask for your blessings and guidance on this Peace Journey.

We center now in our hearts the three fold flame of Wisdom, Love and Power connecting to the Source of never ending perfection, the Heart and Mind of Mother/Father God. We radiate the Wisdom, Love, and Power of God into the opening of this Stargate projecting the blessings of limitless Peace, Love and Abundance to each and every one on Earth.

The opening of this Stargate creates a grid of Divine Peace and Love uniting the fifth dimensional Pleiadian Christ Consciousness of every embodied soul. Through our I AM Presence we consecrate this journey. Divine Love and Peace will now flow eternally blessing all life on Earth.

Beloved I AM, we are so grateful to Chief Joseph and St. Germain for seeding these Stargates 10,000 years ago and creating this path in 1877. Humbly we thank you for this transformational journey and all its blessings.

Beloved I AM, we are so grateful to activate God's Power on Earth through these Stargates and we are humbled before His magnificent Presence.

Beloved I AM, we are so grateful for our gift of Life and our ability to add Light to the world.

Beloved I AM, we are so grateful that we are open doors that no one can shut.

Beloved I AM, we are so grateful for God's infinite Abundance and Eternal Peace.

Beloved I AM, we are so GRATEFUL!

Our I AM Presence now activates specific DNA codes containing the Immaculate Concept for each of our Divine Purpose and reason for being. We are stepping into the doorway of multi-dimensional Reality. We are fully ascended and illumined. Our life now reflects in all ways the Immaculate Concept of Eternal Peace, Love and unlimited Abundance.

We bring into our hearts the Golden Ray of Melchizedek and the Ray of Sananda allowing the full momentum of blessings into our every day life experiences. These Rays pour through our hearts into the Heart of Mother Gaia. Reaching this Stargate they flood every particle of life with Abundance and Eternal Peace. Now ascending from the heart of Mother Gaia back through our heart, the Rays return to Source, Mother/Father God. We radiate the Ray of Eternal Peace in all we do to all Life on Earth. The entire planet is now enfolded in the Golden Light of Eternal Peace. From this day and this moment forward, every thought, word, action or feeling we express shall be qualified with the Golden Light of Eternal Peace and Divine Love. With every breath we are an open portal for the full magnitude of the gifts from these Rays. Thank You Lord Melchizedek and Lord Sananda. We accept the opening of this sacred Stargate gloriously accomplished through the power of God, I AM. And so it is.

We had laid out my sacred prayer blanket monogrammed with the symbol OM. So fitting—this was before we knew our pilgrimage would be called Journey OM. I had spent many, many hours of yoga and meditation on my special blanket. Woven within the threads was the vibration of these many hours with God.

Next we brought out the three precious alchemical singing bowls, each made from precious gemstones and pure quartz crystal. I had no idea why when I purchased them. It was an extravagance at the time, but it was out of my hands. Unbeknownst to me they were an integral part of this calling. They came to me out of the blue immediately after our trip to Mount Shasta at the exact moment I received an unexpected check for the exact amount of the purchase. The platinum bowl tuned to the Divine Mother, the indium blue bowl connecting to the dolphin energy and my favorite, the ruby bowl, connecting to the heart of Jesus/Lord Sananda.

I should mention that I am connected to the mineral kingdom. For me they are the true joining of Earth to the celestial realms. They are my Heaven on Earth; As Above, So Below. The mineral kingdom carries the vibration and frequencies found in the higher celestial realm. They mirror the essence of the Sacred Rays. At times we cannot integrate this high celestial vibration. We are not evolved to the point of holding this Light quotient and until we are attuned our energy system would simply "short out." The beauty of the mineral kingdom is that it holds the same vibrational essence of the Sacred Rays only in a stepped down physical form that we can use. Just as each Ray carries an aspect of God—Love, Illumination, Will, Peace, Transformation, and so on—each rock, mineral and crystal also holds a specific vibration. This is why they are such useful healing tools. Using the stones for a specific purpose allows us to connect with the appropriate energy necessary to clear blocks in our energy system, raise our awareness and awaken to enlightenment. We simply choose which stone corresponds with the specific energy frequency needed to help us with the issue or lesson we are facing. I have assembled an entire line called Synergy Stones™ that do just that.

I have many favorites. For our pilgrimage I chose three stones, or more correctly, they chose to go with me. A year ago at Kehoe's Rock shop in Big Fork, Montana I had found a double terminated amethyst point. Until now it was lovely to look at but it hadn't found its purpose. Suddenly it was perfectly clear—this special crystal would be my direct line to Chief Joseph and St. Germain. I would wear it in a leather pouch around my neck; it would remain with me always throughout the entire trip. It became especially useful transmuting all misqualified energy along our way.

The second stone was one just recently given to me, a gift I received from Watsu Master, Dave. During a Watsu session a month before our departure Dave handed me a stone and told me someone had left it earlier that week with the message it was for someone who would be coming to his lagoon. Neither the giver nor Dave knew who this person would be. It was for me, Shima. For the next month I worked with this special stone trying to unlock its secrets. I slept with it, meditated with it, talked to it. And then I went to Ahriah:

The stone comes from the moon. It is a Moon Mother Stone. It was given to many, many generations of matriarchal lineages of the Pleiadian Star women. It is a leadership stone in terms of leading the body into ascension and leading the body into these vortexes and Stargates that would reassemble the physical, mental, and emotional bodies back into their sacred geometry. Take the stone with you. It is your stone. It was originally given to you by the moon Mothers and by that we mean Isis herself.

The stone is unlocking much within you. It will continue to reveal to you especially as you move into this journey. Take it with you. People that see the stone will remember it and will remember you by it. In essence it is a note of confirmation of who you are and also a historic key and representative from the Moon Mothers. It will be honored.

The third stone was a spherical polished piece of petrified wood, reddish in color with a white center looking very much like a goddess. I had picked up this stone at my friend Velvet's store, *Rocks and Things Metaphysical* in Whitefish. Velvet is pure light innocence, a gifted reflexologist who combines several modalities in a unique healing touch. In a session with her last summer we awakened a past life memory of my life as a Ute medicine woman in Southern Utah in the early 1800s, very close to the time and place of my life with Chief Joseph and the Nez Perce. It was a sacred moment of reconnecting and in retrospect a key to this journey connecting me to my medicine woman wisdom and powers.

I chose an essential oil for each Stargate. Through our five senses we can connect energetically to our higher selves. We've all experienced the uplifting of our spirits and the fond remembrance of joyful times through the power of smell. Each essential oil holds a unique vibration pattern and by infusing the aroma of specially chosen oil we can connect to the vibration of each Stargate. And in Native American tradition we always blessed and thanked Mother Earth and our Ancestors with sacred leaf tobacco and blue cornmeal. Judith had given me sacred soil from her home in Chimayo, New Mexico. It is most powerful connecting to the One.

We took a piece of sacred ash given to me by my friend, Dave, and rubbed it on the palm of our left hand to open to the Wisdom and Unity of the coalition of all the Native American Elders and Spiritual Leaders. This ash is from the sacred fires of the Northwest Council, a gathering of all tribes coming together in the spirit of unity and celebration. Dave had the privilege of attending this sacred ceremony a few years ago and was gifted some of the sacred ash from the fire. Along with the Mother Moon Stone and the sacred ash he is very much a part of this calling.

And lastly my favorite, the waters, the Peace Waters and the Holy Water of Lourdes. I am Shima, Peace Goddess of the Waterways. This is not my given name in this lifetime. That name was Darcy. Darcy served me well carrying the vibration and the energy necessary to move through my childhood and excel in the corporate world. Now I have returned to my soul heritage. Shima is the primal vibration of my soul. I have returned through all of the worlds and all of the civilizations back to this primal vibration which is Shima. My soul lineage is through the Elohim Peace. The name Shima is the combination of the words, Shanti (Peace), Elohim and Aloha. I express myself through Peace through the waterways. We bless ourselves and the site of the Stargate with the holy water from Lourdes and the Peace Waters from Whitefish.

Ceremony complete at the opening of *Ancient Wisdom,* we cover the sacred bundle with a branch appropriately shaped like a three-legged dog. It's a family joke and symbolic to us of Jim's affinity for three-legged dogs and my bringing three-legged dogs home. The beginnings of the song "Waneen Wan Yan" emerged. Jim liked my simple song; it would carry us the rest of the way unveiling verse by verse as we carried on Stargate to Stargate. Journey On.

Opening Stargates is an energizing experience. We are instantly catapulted into the celestial realm of pure joy—timeless and limitless. The fatigue from the day's activities before opening *Ancient Wisdom* vanished in a flash and we were left refreshed and energized, happily on our way back across Hell's Canyon to spend the night in the small town of Lewiston, Idaho. After time in the sparsely populated areas of Oregon, Lewiston felt like the big city. And it had a Starbucks!

We had reservations at the Holiday Inn Express. Greeted by Michelle who announced this was her first night on the job so she was supervised closely by Angie, a spunky sixty-year-old "here to please." Angie wore an Alexandrite ring; we struck up a conversation. This is a stone I was told over a year ago would come my way, that it would hold special significance for me. The magic of Alexandrite is in the shifting of its colors from red-purple to blue-green when different wavelengths of Light shine upon it. It is a high vibrational stone of intense wisdom and heart energy. It reminds us the pure joy of the celestial realms is always here for us and it is simply the level we choose to receive that creates our reality in that moment. I have been on the lookout for my Alexandrite ring. Here I had found it. Not exactly the finger I was expecting to see it on, but God didn't fill in that part!

We checked into a welcome and clean room. Finding food was not as easy, so we settled for an old style pizza parlor before franchises were popular. Jim remarked he could still envision the cigarette vending machine with the old fashioned pull knobs in the restaurant doorway. I guess that was his first experience with smoking. He was also intrigued by the kitchen with an observation deck and Plexiglas windows where patrons could watch their food being prepared. The first of its kind back in the day, I doubt they had the electronic fly zapper as part of their equipment. I ordered spaghetti marinara. No meat they said, but made with meat flavoring. Yes, I felt like I was back home growing up in Billings, Montana. Some things never change in the Western United States. A young girl, no older than 10 and bored sitting with her parents, entertained us with her gymnastics on the viewing platform rails. We encouraged her; Jim determined she was setting out to be a future pole dancer. After a restful night in Lewiston we journeyed on in our dreams.

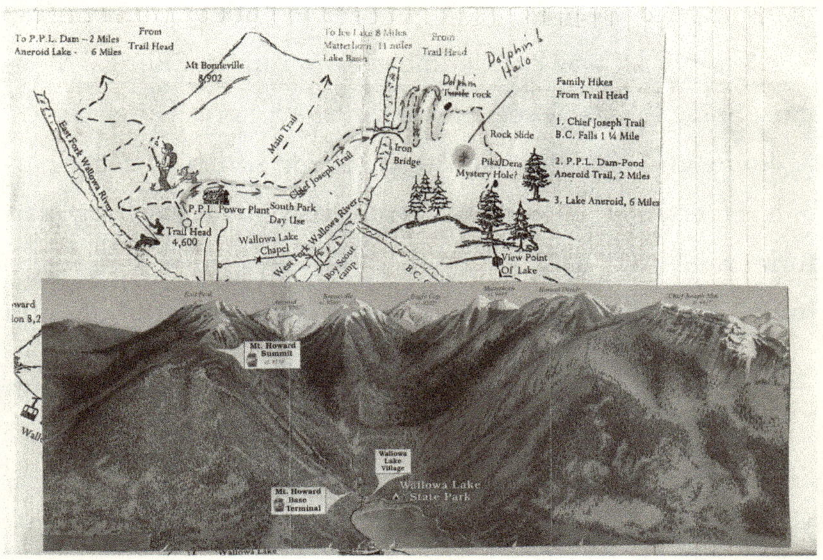
To P.P.L. Dam – 2 Miles
Aneroid Lake – 6 Miles
From
Trail Head
Mt Bonneville
8,902
To Ice Lake 8 Miles
Matterhorn 11 miles
Lake Basin
From
Trail Head
Dolphin's
Halo
Dolphin rock
Family Hikes
From Trail Head
1. Chief Joseph Trail
B.C. Falls 1 ¼ Mile
2. P.P.L. Dam-Pond
Aneroid Trail, 2 Miles
3. Lake Aneroid, 6 Miles
East Fork Wallowa River
Main Trail
Chief Joseph Trail
Iron
Bridge
Rock Slide
Pika Dens
Mystery Hole?
P.P.L. Power Plant
South Park
Day Use
Trail Head
4,600
Wallowa Lake
Chapel
West Fork Wallowa River
Boy Scout
camp
View Point
Of Lake
Mt. Howard
Summit
Wallowa
Lake
Village
Wallowa Lake
State Park
Mt. Howard
Base
Terminal

Lostine Campsite

At the junction of the Lostine and Wallowa Rivers is a traditional Nez Perce summer campsite where Old Chief Joseph died in 1871. This landscape has changed little from the days before the area was settled. ***Not a developed site.***

no information

Old Chief Joseph Me… and Gravesite

This is a national historic landmark and sacred site dedicated to *Tuekakas*, Old Chief Joseph. He is referred to as Old Joseph to distinguish him from his son, Chief Joseph *(Hinmatooyalahtqit.)* As a young man, *Tuekakas* converted to Christianity. Old Joseph signed the treaty of 1855, which set aside 7 million acres for the Nez Perce Reservation. Eight years later, he refused to sign a new treaty that relinquished more than 6 million acres.

Old …

The … 1926. Nearby are the graves of other Nez Perce and some settlers.

blessed grave site w/ Peace Water
Sunday, May 24 afternoon

Enterprise

Chief Joseph Monument:

West of downtown Enterprise, an interpretive panel honoring Chief Joseph overlooks the Wallowa Valley, the Wallowa band of the Nez Perce traditional homeland.

Wallowa Mountains Office & Visitor's Center, Wallowa-Whitman National Forest

Open daily 8am-5pm during summer months, Monday-Friday in winter.

Features dioramas of Nez Perce lifeways, maps, and informational literature.

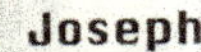

Joseph

The Nez Perce name for this area was *hah-un-sah-pah*—"big rocks lying scattered around." Today, Joseph is a town with homes, shops, and artisan galleries. The streets are 100 feet wide, originally built to accommodate a 4-horse team turnabout. South of Joseph, near scenic Wallowa Lake, is the symbolic beginning of the Nez Perce flight of 1877.

stone people
get encodements

5/24 Sunday
afternoon

pine cone

Joseph is known as "Big Rocks Scattered Around". These rocks are stone people, stone beings. Make personal contact with the rocks. Some of the places you will receive encodements. Go around and touch as many as you can. Make a tobacco offering to them.

Sunday afternoon 6/23
a huge lone pine stands guard – rocks lie everywhere – holding wisdom from time immemorial. We gave blessings of corn meal + tobacco. Blessed w/ the nourishing Peace Waters + grounded of the soil of sacred Chimayo NM. The river rushes nearby – the wind of spirit rejuvenates.

Asotin

Nez Perce called the creek that flows into the Snake River near present day Asotin, Washington *Héesutine*, or "eel creek." This was the winter camp of Looking Glass' nontreaty band. Asotin, Washington is six miles south of Clarkston, Washington. River boat trips are available from here.

4 Trees - Guardians / Ancestors on way to Spalding

Ancient Wisdom

Wise Old Tree

2. ~~Joseph Cave~~ – Magenta Ray

Sunday May 24 5:00 pm
Stargate
Joseph Cave

Joseph Canyon Viewpoint
The canyon seen from the overlook was one of the winter homes of the Nez Perce. Tradition holds that Chief Joseph was born in a cave along the east bank of the creek. Restrooms are available seasonally.

Joseph Canyon Viewpoint

Nez Perce called this area *saqánma*, which means "long, rough canyon." This dramatic viewpoint on Oregon State Highway 3, about 38 miles north of Enterprise, shows where families of the Wallowa band made their winter camps, at the confluence of Joseph Creek and Grande Ronde River.

mountain harebell bellflower

The timeless winds of the past blow by
Come to whisper around us welcoming
our grandfather "Jim"

Directions: Park @ Joseph Canyon Viewpoint Walk South on West side of road ½ mile turn right thru grove of pine trees Head West you will see an old wise redwood tree no longer living but covered in living moss a giant among trees. Marked by a 3 legged dogwood

Monday, May 25, 2009

We awake at sunrise excited to be on our way. The journey is unfolding and each step leads us to a new adventure, another miracle. We couldn't wait to get started. Three squirrels in three different locations greeted us. They were getting our attention. When a squirrel shows up get ready for coming changes by clearing out anything that no longer serves you. Travel Light! Days prior it had been the robins. Today it was the squirrels. Today's message from the squirrels: play and balance.

Driving along the Snake River nine miles south of Asotin on our way to Buffalo Eddy we came upon a small mountain jutting up from the Snake River in the perfect shape of a pyramid. The river drive was so beautiful we knew there was something here, but had no conscious knowing of what it was. This was the first of three pyramid mountains we would encounter and later we learned there was a gift awaiting us at each one. Jim called it Cleopatra's Bend. We were taken into a state of grace—Oneness. We felt they were holding something for us—our intuition was tuning in. Later we learned that yes, indeed there was a gift awaiting. The most beautiful aspect of this ascension work we have found is the more we give the more we receive.

There are Masters in each one of these mountains holding the Flame of Illumination with Lord Lanto. Lord Lanto is a great Light of ancient China and most recently served as Chohan of the Second Ray, the Flame of Illumination until Lord Kuthumi took over. Lord Lanto's retreat is in the Grand Teton Mountains in Wyoming. Some of his incarnations include the Duke of Chou who is considered the architect of the Chou Dynasty and the true founder of the Confucian tradition. He was a ruler of China at the time of Confucius and held the Flame of Illumination on behalf of the Chinese people for many centuries. He is dedicated to assisting the ascension of our planet through the Cosmic Christ illumination.

The Second Ray, this Flame of Illumination is the Precipitation Flame of Abundance and Wealth, Happiness, Joy and Universal Christ Consciousness. This Ray represents God-Wisdom. The connection streaming through these mountains and the ranges we have been traveling along is all part of the Second Ray of Illumination. Each of these Master Beings in these pyramid mountains was called to hold our energy as a visionary and as an oversouling gift as we passed through.

Each Master Being had a gift of wisdom, first at Cleopatra's Bend in Idaho, then Livingston, Montana, and finally Chinook, Montana. From now on we will look at Pyramid Mountains with new eyes. And lo and behold, two weeks later approaching our home in San Diego we see for the first time a pyramid mountain. Right in our back yard! Yes, we are seeing with new eyes and awakening to the magic of life on this precious planet. Eternal gratitude!

We stopped at Cleopatra's Bend and made offerings. We shared Peace Waters, the Chimayo sacred soil and holy water of Lourdes bringing in the Goddess energy from Mother Mary and all of the feminine deities. It was there that Serapis Bay paid us a visit. Serapis Bay is the Ascended Master from the Ascension Temple in Luxor, Egypt. Twelve thousand years ago he was entrusted with transferring the Ascension Flame to a safe place just before the sinking of Atlantis. His most familiar incarnation was Leonidas, King of Sparta. Many of the ascension temples are on the etheric plane. The Ascension Temple in Luxor however, is located on the physical plane and was opened to mankind in 1952. Serapis Bay is the chohan of the Fourth Ray, the Ascension Flame of Purification. And here he was at Cleopatra's Bend showing us our ascension path. What a gift to receive him in our hearts—and not have to travel to Luxor!

Buffalo Eddy is located along the Snake River 15 miles outside of the town of Asotin, Idaho on Highway 129. Along the banks of the river there are large boulder outcroppings. On the face of the rocks ancient petroglyphs evidence the home and longevity of the Nimiipuu in this area. Most interesting is that the same drawings have been found on five different continents all dating to the same period. We are in awe of the interconnectedness of our world and the unseen powers in form.

We arrived at Buffalo Eddy early Monday morning, May 25th and were immediately greeted by a meadowlark—a sure sign to expect a pleasant surprise. I was told this would be a very important receiving place for us. Here ancient knowledge was encoded in the petroglyph panels. It would be like going to a library. If I were to stand in front of the petroglyph panels and open my 3rd eye I would be encoded with important information, ancient knowledge. Okay then. There is something that will be given to me here. This is very important. Those were my instructions and so with that clue we headed down the path. Terry, the Forest Ranger at the Nez Perce National Historic Park had drawn a simple map for us to follow. He guided us beyond the typical stopping point of tourists and encouraged us to scramble on the rocks and discover the real glyphs hidden from the main trail. And so we did. And the scramble was well worth the effort.

We have entered the sacred library of petroglyphs. It is beyond belief—it takes our breath away. We open to its many gifts giving thanks with corn meal and sacred leaf, bringing in the Divine Mother energy form the Lourdes holy water, the Immaculate Concept—unadulterated, pure. We bless with

Peace Waters Elohim and with pen in hand are open to receive. The sound of the river babbling, flowing, rushing, is a peaceful sound—swift. It is okay to move swiftly, but always with inner calm in the eye of Peace.

I have been here. I remember passing the time away on summer days here, dipping into the river to cool off; drawing pictures on the stone to express God's creativity. I am a child, alive, innocent in the joy of the sun, the water, scrambling on the rocks. I live a life of ease, safe, loved by family and community. I have no worries, no work; all play (as reminded by the squirrel this morning). The Peace flows through me. I am the river of water, river of body, river of life.

Pieces of the ancient stone glyphs have been taken by man to adorn their homes and collections. It is just ignorance. They do not know better, but a simple reminder that there are still veils between Heaven and Earth. We forgive. We allow. There is no space for anything but Love in this area of the Singing Waters. We hold them harmless in God's Light for when they return they will come with the rock pieces and we will forgive them as we forgive ourselves for taking "pieces" along the way. All will come back in perfect symmetry; the One again.

And so a song begins:

Waneen Wan Yan

It is all One

Waneen Wan Yan

Journey Begun

Home to the Sun

Back to the One

Waneen Wan Yan

We are all One

At the point of return Jim noticed the river flowing in both directions, circling in the center, bubbling. North, south, no, going both directions at the same time, a vortex, a portal we see with our own eyes. There is a glyph on the stone walls describing this action. "This is the place where they saw the Ancient Astronauts," Jim says. And I believe. We had gotten into the playful habit of saying "Journey On" whenever we had made a stop and were ready to move on. After the profound gifts bestowed on us at Buffalo Eddy, Singing Waters "Journey On" became "Journey OM." It was symbolic of the elevated state we were tuned into, a fifth dimensional frequency that became the norm. Only when we were catapulted back to third dimension did we revert to journeying on and not OM.

After a healthy picnic lunch in the town park of Asotin surrounded by a gaggle of geese, we prepared to open the next Stargate a few miles out of town at an historical landmark called Ant and Yellow Jacket and Coyote's Fishnet. The story of Coyote's Fishnet goes like this: Coyote and Black Bear got into an argument. In frustration, Coyote threw his fishing net on a hill and tossed Black Bear on another, turning him into stone. The net and the Bear are visible rock outcroppings. Ant and Yellow Jacket got into an argument over who had the right to fish for salmon. Coyote asked them to stop. They continued to fight, whereby Coyote turned them into a stone arch. The arch is now an historical landmark and visible from the scenic turn-out along Highway 12.

In my pilgrimage instructions prior to departing, Lord Melchizedek shared with me that the Stargate which we would open near Coyote Fishnet would be connected to the Stargate *Heart of the Golden Rose*. Opening the *Heart of the Golden Rose* would allow the shadow and Light to integrate and come into wholeness again; that the chain had broken, tricking mankind out of its divinity by miscreating it into form less than pure God Essence. It would allow for all mankind to now stand true and pure, each in their God Essence knowing who they truly are.[5]

Stargate #3 showed how we move out of ego in our planetary spiritual evolution only to be faced with another point of separation when the galactic self comes forward. When the power of our mastery comes back in there is still the danger of misrepresenting the power of God through our own Source energy. This

---

[5] The gift to mankind at the *Heart of the Golden Rose* Stargate is similar to the benefit received from *Swallows Window*. However, it goes a step further in our spiritual evolution. We will never be truly free of temptation and misperception until we are fully merged into one with God. Until then our lessons will continue, albeit easier and lighter, and we will respond with greater wisdom and knowing. Our falls won't be quite so steep and the landing not quite so hard. But it is naïve to think we will be free of a misstep now and again as long as we have free will.

is another place of rectification, of reconstitution and re-contextualization. I am beginning to realize the ascension process never really ends. First is planetary, then solar, galactic, cosmic and universal. The Ascended Masters have willingly offered their assistance to move through this stage of spiritual evolution in our ascension process.

The Great Divine Director has promised to work with us at this Stargate to assure the symmetry of the Mahatma Energy synthesis comes through, that it will be brought to Divine Order and not misused through the galactic self. The Mahatma, unlike the Ascended Masters we know, can best be described as a synthesis of energy, not an individual energy source. It is the highest vibration the Earth can hold at this time. The Great Divine Director is a Great Cosmic Being who has authority for the conditions of Earth. The Divine Director observes each of us and at a certain point when we can be of assistance to mankind he determines which miscreations can be transmuted. He has for more than 200,000 years assisted life streams to perfect the outer manifestation of their self. We can summon the Great Divine Director to set us free from the pressure of human creation and therefore transmute and liberate us of our own human miscreation. He is the Teacher of Saint Germain and El Morya. St. Germain worked under him in a similar manner as Jesus worked with Lord Maitreya. So you see even as we ascend it is never fully complete. It is yet another step on the ascension ladder. But it does become easier, more blissful and we do experience Heaven on Earth.

When we arrived at the scenic turnout we could see the rock outcroppings. They were on a steep mountainside overlooking the highway—clearly not the site of the Stargate. We sat in the car and scratched our heads wondering, "Where do we look?" What do we know about this Stargate? It's of the Diamond Ray and holds a geometric code that organizes the sacred geometry and Light fields. The activation tone is "eeeennnn" the second syllable of Waneen. It aligns with the 3rd eye and is oversouled by Sanat Kumara.

The Ascended Master Sanat Kumara is a Hierarch of Venus and is the Regent Lord of the World. Eighteen and a half million years ago during Earth's darkest hour, Sanat Kumara came to Earth to keep the threefold flame alight on behalf of mankind. He offered humanity the most selfless act of Love by becoming a voluntary exile for millions of years from his home planet Venus, and away from his beloved twin flame Venus, the goddess of Love and Beauty. He held the Light for humanity who could no longer supply it for themselves.

I am baffled. I can't find anything in this that will show us the way. I know it is not possible to find a Stargate through the mind by thinking and that's exactly what I'm trying to do. Until now, since we departed Spokane on Saturday, there had been no cell coverage, email communication, no news from the outside world. We were totally immersed in our "God calling" and truly in another dimension. At that moment my phone rang. I wouldn't answer; a disturbance I thought and nothing that could be more important than what I was presently doing.

Jim said, "See who it is. It could be a message." Begrudgingly, I answered. And it was—another helper in the form of Ahriah. Just as I was answering the phone I looked up to see a raven fly over and land on the Ant and Yellow Jacket outcropping. I'd been getting into my head and farther and farther away from my heart. Since I had Ahriah on the phone I thought "if I could just connect through channeling I would get the next puzzle piece to continue." It's important to know that Ahriah works on a schedule. She is not prone to spontaneity. She takes her work very seriously and never "just connects" to the Ascended Master realm without ceremonial preparation. But what the heck, it's worth a try. Remember? *CliffsNotes.* And so I ask. Yes! She is free to talk. And the next gift of understanding unfolds:

> *This area holds the energy of misusing our power when all of the gifts of enlightenment come back. It is the integration point of the Mahatma (synthesis) energy into the physical body. All the layers are coming back into order. There is no longer one part of us saying, "I'm going back" and another part saying "I'm going forward." No longer will we experience the internal dialogue chattering, "I'm holier than you and I know more than you." This site holds numerous energies of paradox—duality.*

In Native American lore the Coyote is the trickster and the Black Bear is power. When and where do we trick ourselves in and out of rightful power? Here is the Coyote seeing his faults and trying to get Yellow Jacket and Ant to stop fighting; he sees there's no way out and it will end badly. After the opening of this Stargate, there will be no place for trickery.

But where is it? I am drawn to a grove of trees about a quarter mile off to the right of the Ant and Yellow Jacket arch. The raven landed on Ant and Yellow Jacket which would typically signal to us to go there, but there's no way to reach the rock outcropping. It is too high and too steep. I have learned that Stargates are beautiful and serene. This rock outcropping is harsh, noisy and impinged by the highway. Not it. This is not the Stargate, but the raven could be the clue to where it is. I see a raven fly by the grove of trees and make a complete circle from Ant and Yellow Jacket to the grove. It is circling the two. Now there are two ravens. When a raven shows up there is magic in the air. Something special is about to happen. It means one is gradually evolving to a more confident, powerful and spiritual being—time to let go of your old self. Precisely the guidance I was given earlier: "If there is anything I am not sure of, let it go now." There's our answer!

Ahriah and I continue:

> *The trees are the sacred Mothers who hold the key to move through the rock arch. The rock symbolizes the removal of obstacles. Once you pass through the Ant and Yellow Jacket arch through the grove of trees any and all physical obstruction blocking the portals back into Light will be removed. There will be no place for error.*

The raven is telling us, like the sphinx, that the grove of trees holds the sacred secret and it's the key to opening the energy to these mysteries. At prior Stargates we'd always found an entrance or key; the rock arch and the grove of trees are this entrance. I ask, "Do Mahatma, Melchizedek and Sanat Kumara play a part in this Stargate? I feel their energy so strongly."

Yes, Sanat Kumara came back to Earth to rectify all of mis-creation; to pull Earth out of its inevitable destruction if it were to continue on the same downward spiraling path. Melchizedek brings in the sacred Laws. The Divine Director makes the Laws flow and Mahatma synthesizes it all so there is no obstruction. After you open this Stargate there will be no place for error. There will be no block between your inter-dimensional selves. This will be the hardest Stargate for you to open for you are freeing yourself as well as mankind in this process. If there is anything in you that you are not sure of yourself, let it go! Now! That is why they are making you work a little harder.

We hang up and Jim and I chuckle. Reminiscent of the television show, *Who Wants to Be a Millionaire?* This was "Call a Friend." Our Stargate lifeline! Journey OM. We head to the grove of trees. There is a gravel road, Coyote Gulch Road. "This is it," I tell Jim. Traveling along the dusty, washboard road we come to a hillside. Hundreds and hundreds of swallows nests mark the hillside. Flying above us is a swirl of swallows, thousands flying in a circle; a vortex of swallows. A swallow brings the message that it is time to let go and move on; the same message I had heard from Lord Melchizedek a short while earlier, *"If there is anything I am not sure of, let it go now."* The swallow guides us to release old issues and wounds. The swallow shows up if there might be turbulence ahead assuring us we will be able to ride it out. Another premonition of what was ahead at Souls Knolls. The swallow provides protection and guidance during periods of darkness, again unknowingly preparing us for our next stop.

We pull over. We have never seen anything like this. Yes, we've seen the swallows at San Juan Capistrano and under the interstate bridge at Lake Hodges, but never anything like this. We are enraptured! We open the car door to get out and get a closer look and there below the swallows nests, littered along the ground, are hundreds and hundreds of shotgun shell casings. A sobering duality, but that is why we are here. Our purpose in opening this Stargate is to merge all into Oneness, to rectify all miscreation and bring everything back into the Light.

Across from Swallows Hill is another hillside, bigger, but not big enough to be called a mountain. It is covered in spring grass and wildflowers. On the face of the hill are rock tailings, geometric designs where no vegetation grows. They look like symbols and I know them on a subconscious level. I don't know what they say, but I know they are glyphs. They remind me of the Ascension Keys symbols. Some even look like the petroglyphs at Singing Waters. I remember now this Stargate is the Diamond Ray and that the Diamond Ray holds the geometric codes which organize the sacred Light field. Light Language; Geometric glyphs; Diamond Ray. Now my heart is back to leading the way and it all starts to make sense.

We climb a steep hill and begin the ceremony to open this Stargate. It is hot, the climb is steep and it takes more effort than we expected to even find this place. Once we settled in, the sun seems less stifling, a cool breeze picks up and the insects give us space. Yes, we found the Stargate, perched above the Swallows Hill and in direct line with the glyphs on the hillside. But we weren't finished with the duality. Not yet. As I played the singing bowls and began the holy consecration of ourselves and the land a car drove by. We were in the middle of nowhere, seven miles in on a gravel road, no farmhouses, nothing in sight. The car stopped right below us. We were too high for them to see us, but our car was parked below. Jim held guard; I was distracted. Another disturbance; I moved into fear, afraid of being asked what we were doing. Are we trespassing? Are they going to break into our car? We pause. They pass. I regain my Peace and continue. Duality dissolved. After opening *Swallows Window* we sit in silence. The sky was brilliant blue, not a cloud to be seen "for as far as the eye could see." As Jim lay staring into space he watched a huge cloud form above him. In a twinkling of an eye he saw it grow bigger and bigger and get closer and closer. He pointed to it, not believing his eyes. I nonchalantly stated, "Oh, that's a starship."[6] In a flash it disappeared. If you know Jim, you know among his greatest gifts is discernment. He is supreme at judging character; my ultimate protector, guide, companion, and now Scout. But along with this incredible gift of discernment comes critical judgment. Just like Doubting Thomas, until he puts his finger through the nail wounds of Jesus, he won't believe the Master stands before him.

Out of pure Love for me, Jim has always gone along with my feelings, my knowing, my unique way of seeing life. He never judges, but I know he can hardly believe the things I oftentimes share with him. When Jim saw the starship, it was an "Aha!" moment for him. It could not be denied. He had just put his finger in the wound of Jesus. I am told Jim will be given many concrete experiences as we move on because his doubting nature requires the practical application of physical sight and touch. At this juncture, seeing was believing and we Journey OM.

Our next stop is Lenore, a portal to the Ancestor Spirits. It is a place where the ancients could travel between dimensions back to Earth after having left its physical plane. For reasons unknown, perhaps misuse, it had been closed; now was the

---

[6] I had my first experience of starships last summer at Lake Louise at the etheric temple of Archangel Michael and the initial amazement had worn off. Since then I had became more and more accustomed to living inter-dimensionally, recognizing and acknowledging our extraterrestrial brothers and sisters.

time for reopening, which is what we've been asked to do. Lenore is not a Stargate. It is a portal where the Ancestor Spirits can come once again and guide their people.

The robins had followed us from Whitefish on Saturday morning to the front lawn of Wallowa Lake and back to Lewiston. Jim had connected deeply to their energy. Never far away, they guided us on our way Saturday, Sunday and Monday mornings. Then the three squirrels took over, at least until lunch in Lenore on Monday afternoon. Then the robins returned in a big way. Before we began our ceremony to open this portal we picnicked by the river near a grove of trees. It was lovely and restful after a long day. As we packed up our picnic supplies, being a bit tired, I suggested that "just our presence," our energy alone would open this portal, no ceremony necessary. In spiritual jargon this is being lazy. Yes, our energy fields do have an effect, but it's never the same as bringing in the Ascended Masters and Emissaries of Light and consciously opening the portal. Nevertheless, I rationalized that, after all, this isn't a Stargate, so we'll just take a few photos and be on our way. We started walking around the park looking for the ideal photo opportunity. We were drawn to two trees, one iridescent lime green and the other a shimmering aspen. Two trunks, two species, but in an odd way they appeared as one. One, just like us I thought.

As I stepped forward, my foot in midair, I looked down to see a bright neon yellow spot. "What an unusual flower," I thought. It was opening before my eyes. I drew my foot back just in time to discover it was a baby robin, so well camouflaged he could only be seen when he opened his mouth exposing an exquisite other worldly fluorescent yellow. Next to the baby robin was another baby and another—three baby robins had fallen from their nest. It appeared they had been there most of the day, not long enough for a predator to make them their meal, but very weak and barely hanging on. One baby had died, most likely from the fall from the nest, leaving two babies still alive—but not for long. Now we could hear Mother Robin off a short distance. She was frantic and so was I! "We must save them," I cried. "Too late," Jim simply stated. "Let nature takes it course. There is nothing we can do." He rationalized that they had been on the ground too long and were near death. No, we couldn't take them with us and we must let nature take its course. Looking up into the pine tree we could see the nest. It was out of reach, but not too far. The winds had been strong the night before. Could they have dislodged it? A predator, perhaps, or three rambunctious babies just getting too big for their home? Whatever, we had two stranded babies and a nest that, with a little effort, just might be reachable. Grabbing the ice chest I cajoled Jim into climbing as far as he could to set the nest right. The least we could do was get them into their nest to help soothe Mother Robin. After a bit of clamoring Jim was able to right the nest and secure it; one by one we lifted the tiny birds back into the home. We received thanks immediately, little chirps; although weak from a day on the ground, they sang their gratitude.

But we weren't done. We took the tiny bird having died from the fall to the rushing river. With Peace Waters and prayers we released him down the river. On our return up the river bank we could hear Mother Robin chirping nearby. Apparently she had been trying to keep her babes alive on the ground and was now even more distraught to find them missing. Within a few minutes, mother and babies were united. Hopefully, the next time the nest tilts they'll be ready to fly.

We still weren't done! A blessing beyond blessing was ready to be bestowed. Intent on taking the pictures of the "Two as One" trees for our journal we picked up where we left off. As we walked, Jim shared a story:

> *I remember being no older than five, maybe four. I wasn't in school yet and it was before I could read or write. I think we lived in Boston. In the front yard was a tree; I loved playing on the front porch running back and forth to that tree. Even then I had a fascination for climbing trees. One day I had scrambled up as far as my courage would take me and discovered a robin's nest. Inside were two sky blue eggs. I was mesmerized; I must show my mom! Carefully, ever so carefully, I lifted the eggs one by one and gently placed them in my pocket. I shimmied down the tree and ran to the front porch barely able to hold back my excitement. I reached into my pocket only to discover the eggs were smashed. I was shocked, shamed, heartbroken and fearful of the reprimand awaiting me if I revealed what I had done. So I created a cover-up, a secret held until this moment some 52*

years later triggered by the rescue of the baby robins. The memory released a flood of emotion. Why, at such a young age was I so afraid of punishment? What had I done to know such fear, to know the feeling of such sorrow for breaking the baby eggs?

Together Jim and I recited the breaking of the vows affirmation, releasing all past miscreation. The Love between us burst further open and our hearts sang for saving the baby birds, but more so for the return of the soul fragment that had been torn from this innocent little boy so many years ago. Jim entered that "reality" of authority, punishment and reprimand. With the help of St. Germain and the Violet Flame he was able to transmute all of the misqualified energy he'd carried for so very long. He had come full circle—death to life, predator to savior, ignorance to wisdom. Gift Given, Gift Received. And I thought there was no ceremony to be done! Our hearts were opened and so was the portal at Lenore. Journey OM.

We had stumbled upon a bit of heaven among Best Western motels, the elegant Hearthstone Lodge. Nestled in the mountains outside of Kamiah we discovered down comforters, priceless antiques, deep Jacuzzi baths, plush terry robes and all the amenities of a five-star destination.

It's a beautiful area, rivers running, soft maternal mountains, fair weather and a bed and breakfast inn among the finest to be found anywhere in the world. We learned quickly this area, Kamiah, represents duality, the paradox, the separation of Oneness, what *appears* to be and what *is*—paradise and yet, NOT!

The proprietor, Hardy welcomed us with pride. He paraded us through the lodge showing off his prized collection of French antiques, the library and every detail of construction. He lived in the past when he owned a B&B in Seal Beach, California and was now trying to recreate fonder times in this wilderness. His wife Marjorie clearly ran the show. She came out in full regalia. "We are Christians," she announced as if stating her name. And thus it began, a conversation about Jesus alone being the Savior. I joined in, searching to find common ground for God, too, is everything to me. Like a stern headmistress I was reprimanded. Jesus, the SAVIOR was the only way, not God. God the Father had just taken a demotion. To Marjorie, Chief Joseph and his people were "rebels" but perhaps, just perhaps, because he had been baptized, even though he had fallen away (understandably after his people's land had been stolen from underneath him in the name of white man's God) he may be allowed into heaven. Jesus was clearly the GOD above even God our Father. Feeling the need for approval from this strict disciplinarian, I ran to the car and pulled out my Jesus card which had been traveling with us to show that I, too, was a believer. Too little too late—Marjorie had already labeled me a Liberal. She ranted on for awhile about Obama, Liberals, and the moral and economic destruction of our country. Having had enough, I cut her off. Her parting words were to inform me that the Conservatives were not trying to shut up the Liberals as the Liberals were intent on doing to the Conservatives.

We were given our choice of rooms. As we entered the first room the choice was clear. There at bedside was a picture, an antique print from Prague of a beautiful Goddess. She was holding a baby bird in her hand and two in her lap. There was no mistaking—the Goddess had returned with the baby robins from Lenore. God's way of talking to us always takes my breath away: "Oh ye of little Faith!" No need to look at the second room, but Hardy prided in showing off his antiques so we indulged. Back in the first room we settled in for a refreshing soak in the Jacuzzi and a good night's rest.

When Hardy learned we were following the Chief Joseph Trail he offered to introduce me to Robin, a Forest Service guide and expert on the Nez Perce people. At first I declined, "No thanks," but after a bath and Jacuzzi, clean clothes and a fresh perspective I opened to the idea and asked Hardy to make the introduction. Changing my mind from "no thanks" to "okay" would turn out to be the greatest lesson of the entire journey and a life lesson for me.

Hardy made the introduction and a phone call ensued. One and one-half hours later my head was spinning. This guy, an anthropologist and historian, was a walking encyclopedia and yet, paradoxically, he could not write. Our conversation began with a download of information on the Nez Perce culture; then the conversation turned to Hitler and people's misperception of him and his likeness to Chief Joseph. I followed his line of thinking and listened without judgment. This was not what I was looking for so I tried to steer the conversation to the mystical aspects of the Nez Perce, the shamans and their healing gifts, their connection to the stars. Robin didn't want to go there, but acknowledged it could be. For my sake, "so I could understand" he called the shamans "witches" and for over an hour a puzzling conversation, a non-stop rhetoric like listening to the history channel, ensued. Jim put up his guard and finally cut the conversation off. It was clear I was unaware of who I was talking to.

Afterward, Jim reminded me we were in the land of white supremacy. I was in its face and didn't recognize it. Oftentimes, I am blinded by Oneness and Love; I struggle with the reality of a dark side. My protector, I am so blessed to have Jim at my side. I see now why this particular Stargate will be seeded, but I can't imagine it will be activated or actualized any time soon. Jim says not for the next 5,000 years! I hope for all of our sake he is wrong. The proprietor Hardy masked his truth—a false truth. A soft spoken, educated man, rather nondescript in a bookish way, he was warm and proud to show off his prized possessions. Marjorie chose to use Jesus as a sword against Light, one of the deepest points of rejection of God we can put forth. We're in a culture that has lost its way in the name of Jesus. It has been misdirected by the trickster, moving "believers" out of their God presence under the guise of Christianity. I realized this pilgrimage has a lot to do with learning to live in heightened awareness, embracing and owning the power of my intuition. Was my higher self guiding me when I first responded, "No thank you," to Hardy offering to introduce me to Robin, or was I being misdirected by my free will? There was a moment of discernment to meet Robin. First, I said "No" and then I said "Yes." It would be another 72 hours before I would learn the price of this critical decision.

Refreshed, happy to be "in town" we jumped back into the car for a quick car wash and a bite to eat. It was 8:04 P.M. when we walked into the bar and grill and ask to be served. "Sorry," we were told, "We close at 8:00 P.M." But, but, but…in Jim's sweet way he asked the waitress within ear shot of the cook, "Could you maybe just drop a basket of fries? And then we'll be on our way." The kitchen jargon, "drop a basket" worked like a charm and they kindly agreed. They turned out to be the best French fries we've ever had and the beginning of "Fry Happy!"

Lenore
For thousands of years, this village site was used by the Nez

Lenore Robins' Nest

This is the portal to the Acestor Spirits. Lenore is a place where there was a portal that the ancients went through. It is to be opened. Lenore is not a stargate. It is a portal to the ancestors. It is where the Ancestor Spirits can come and guide the people again.

W... Prairie
...s a root-gathering place for the Nimiipuu and it was ... September 20, 1805, that Lewis and Clark first met ... Perce. During the 1877 War, the Nimiipuu gathered ...ter the Battle of the Clearwater.

Continued **

Tuesday, May 26, 2009

I awoke at 3:01 A.M. troubled by the call the night before with Robin and the "welcome" conversation with Hardy and Marjorie. I put pen to paper:

> *I am the anomaly Robin spoke of, the different one, the extinct one. Interesting—is this a message for me to remain silent, secret and sacred? The information I had anticipated receiving from Robin certainly came in a different package with a very different message. It left me unsure and uneasy. Robin appeared kind. I felt he had an inner sense of knowing, although it appeared flawed somehow, like a veil shrouding the truth. He was living in the fog of untruth; his heart was shackled. I felt he wanted to break the chains, but how? We're meeting for breakfast tomorrow morning at 7:00, then off to open the 4th Stargate at the Heart of the Monster.*

As I tire from journaling, nearly 4:00 A.M. by now, I tell myself my answers only come from within and from my etheric Masters, not from humankind. I drift off to sleep asking for guidance from my Pleiadian journey friends, from Lord Sananda, St. Germain, Chief Joseph and Lord Father Melchizedek for what awaits me in the morning. I must rise above the veils of Earth and not try to save the Marjories, the Hardys, and the Robins of the world. My calling is from God and no one in this place understands the Truth as God has shown me. This place is where people found God and lost Spirit. Some here chose to use Jesus' energy as a sword against Light, a long story but the background for how important it is to open the Stargate at the Heart of the Monster. I sleep. Sunrise is an hour away.

When we checked in the previous afternoon, Hardy excitedly told us about an abandoned culvert under the highway where we could make our way to a place he called "Pebble Beach." Like a small child with a secret passageway he described the route; so naturally, early the next morning we thought it would be a perfect place for our morning meditation. We found the entrance without any trouble, and yes, just as he described, there was a culvert five feet in diameter. The inside of the culvert was dark, but at the end of the tunnel the morning light shined through revealing the river ahead. We made our way through the secret entrance which opened to a small beach, a swift moving river and the morning sunrise—simply beautiful. The air is crisp, cool, a three-layer kind of morning. The sun is bright hinting at what is to come as the day unfolds and the heat sets in. A swallow flies by, linking *Swallows Window* to the next Stargate we are to open at Heart of the Monster. We sit in contemplation. Like a metronome, a heart beat, beautiful bud fronds from a tree swollen with Spring's growth keep time as we sit—timekeepers dropping into the water and floating in perfect rhythm, perfect harmony. This was not a place for closed eye meditation. The beauty was too great.

We bless the river with Peace Waters asking our Creator of All That Is to bring all back into the Immaculate Concept and the Universal Laws of Truth. This was a place of disillusion. Here we were in the most beautiful expansive country, yet with the most limited concept of Life. "Dear God, help me see with perfect, pure, crystal clarity."

We met Robin for breakfast. And yes, to confirm Jim's suspicions from last night's phone call, he met the description. He wore a signet ring on his left pinkie which drew my attention. He was polite, knowledgeable, answered our questions in a circuitous manner, never veering from his script, occasionally alluding to our interests when I caught him off guard with my prompts. He would not make eye contact with me, intent on speaking only to Jim. Both Jim and I tried to get him to connect with me. I was invisible. I was only a voice to ask the question; Jim to receive the answer—fascinating in a quizzical way. When souls are locked like his they cannot make eye contact because the eyes are windows of the soul. Robin's eyes were brown pools from the abyss—no reflection, no light. In our way, Robin and I both overlooked our differences and found common ground, the Nez Perce. We each chose not to believe the truth of the other. He, me, I, he—he was a guide, a helper, on many levels. Or was he? Perhaps so, as everything is always in Divine Order, but perhaps just not who God and my Ascended Master teachers would have chosen for me. I have learned the Masters will never interfere in my free will and as Chief Joseph pointed out on our trip from day one, all paths eventually lead home. Robin led us to Souls Knolls. It was not in our plan and proved to be the Broken Sequence.

All of the events leading up to the opening of the *Heart of the Golden Rose* were rooted in delusion, paradox and duality. For example, the Hearthstone Lodge, a beautiful, pristine place, a jewel among jewels, but entirely out of place as a first-class urban European bed and breakfast in the heart of wilderness where campers, RVs and roadside motels were the norm. Hardy reliving Seal Beach; Marjorie finding Jesus and losing Spirit; the grill open at 7:59 and closed at 8:04. And Robin simply lost.

The story of the Heart of the Monster is a Nez Perce parable. As the story goes long ago there had been a great flood. All the land, people, and animals had been washed away. The flood was the monster. All that remained was the basalt core of the mountain present before the flood. This was the heart of the monster. It symbolizes the battle between the ego and that which is known as the "trickster" for the confirmation of God. Before we left on the pilgrimage I was informed this Stargate would be a particularly potent site for humanity. Opening this Stargate would allow the shadow and the Light a full integration into wholeness again. Humans have been tricking themselves out of their divinity. This Stargate would provide the pathway for those soul extensions to return home again.

Aligned with the solar plexus chakra, it is the Golden Ray of Melchizedek. The activation tone is "Waneen," the point where all consonants and vowels come together. This Stargate will bring the field into harmonic continuum integrating all into wholeness and Oneness. Lord Melchizedek can be looked at as the CEO/President of our Universe. However, he prefers to be considered Father for it connotes abundant Love, sacrifice, strength; the one to be counted on. He holds the highest of all positions in the Spiritual Hierarchy of our Universe. When we pray to "God our Father" it is Lord Melchizedek to whom we pray. It gets a bit confusing because as "sparks of creation" we are all "little Melchizedeks" and so there are many levels using the name Melchizedek. That which I speak of in this writing is the most high. I understand there are twelve levels of Melchizedek frequency called Merkabahs. The highest vibration Earth has thus far been able to assimilate is the fifth Ray anchored by Light Worker, Alton

Kadamon before he ascended. For full ascension, all twelve levels must be anchored and integrated.

We would not only be opening this Stargate, but seeding it for the time when Earth can hold its highest vibration. Until then it will lay dormant and will be activated by another Light Worker when the time is right. For now, I was to be the bridge, the conduit to bring this twelfth level Melchizedek Ray through me to Mother Gaia. To be this conduit, I had to endure a strenuous physical initiation in order to hold this frequency. I can only describe it as the most intense feeling of electrical current you can imagine. Every nerve, every cell was buzzing. I liken it to what those who are bipolar experience in a manic episode. For days prior to our departure I did not sleep. I was not tired and I could feel the high current coursing through my body. All my life in this incarnation I have sought ascension as fast as I was able. I was always guided to "slow down" and allow the process to unfold. I was told if the Light quotient was increased too rapidly the physical body would not be able to handle it. It would be like an electrocution and could result in a mental breakdown, a stroke, heart attack or death. I now know what the Masters were telling me. Once the integration process was complete I felt my normal self again. Yes, I hold a greater Light quotient, but now assimilated I don't notice the physical symptoms and my body is back as before.

At the Stargate of the *Heart of the Golden Rose* we were able to make a site visit the night before the actual ceremony. This made Jim happy. It helped when we could sit with the energy overnight to determine the Stargate's location. Sometimes it really did feel like looking for a needle in a haystack. Heart of the Monster is a huge basalt obelisk centered in a riverside park. This historical landmark is surrounded by meadows chest high with grasses, green and lush, nourished by the moisture of the river. The park attendant keeps it groomed with his riding mower methodically clearing a new pathway each day in the thick grass, expanding the area for tourists to wander.

On our first site visit we walked each grass pathway exploring and developing a feeling for where we would find the Stargate. In our wanderings we came across a wild rose-bush. It looked as though a stray seed had landed in just the right spot over 20 years ago. It was wild, nourished by the perfect balance of water and sun, and had grown to over 5 feet tall unattended. The weight of the branches caused them to bend back down to the trunk, creating a full circle with open space in the middle. We couldn't help being drawn to this unique rosebush.

Originally we thought the actual basalt mound, the Heart of the Monster, was the Stargate. It was fenced off to the public, but we figured if we arrived early enough, right at sunrise, Jim could scamper up the hill, bury the bundle, and scurry down before being seen. Then we would close with ceremony in the park below. But when we arrived the next morning it didn't feel quite right. The energy didn't seem to be what we were looking for so we started exploring. We had forgotten about the rosebush. The park was acres and acres and it would be unlikely we would stumble upon it again. We chose a path that led us to the river. It was high, its banks overflowing, but not raging like the unwelcome energy of most of the rivers we had encountered during this time of spring runoff. This river was moving swiftly but peacefully. A reminder of the insight from Singing Waters: "It is okay to move swiftly but always with inner calm in the eye of Peace." We chanced upon the rosebush once again and knew through synchronicity this was it. The fourth Stargate is about integrating shadow and Light into Oneness. The circular growth pattern of the rosebush symbolized this unity and synthesis.

Opening the prior three Stargates, we had discovered useful clues that would guide us to the spot of the fourth and future Stargates. First, there would always be an animal, bird, or insect to greet us. Second, there would be a Stargate Keeper or guardian in the form of a rock outcropping, a land formation in the shape of a crescent, or a distinctive tree or vegetation holding the key to the entrance. Finally, when we were at the site of the Stargate there would be a palpable change in the energy. If the wind was blowing it would become still. If there were insects, like mosquitoes, they would be noticeably absent, and if the air was too chilly or too hot it would become temperate. If we were in a crowded location we'd suddenly find ourselves alone.

The bird present to greet us this time was of course, the robin. So far, the robin had been the master guide appearing along the entire way. We were also met by a redwing blackbird and a gaggle of geese. We begin. The spirit is light, joyful, playful and easy. We sing our Waneen Wan Yan song. We open the Stargate. We pray. We play the bowls. The birds accompany and the river holds rhythm. With ceremony, we buried the sacred bundle at the base of the rosebush. It's interesting to note that many of the Stargate locations are in the wilderness and require hiking and off road access; there was no problem with conducting our ceremonies which were quite elaborate given the singing bowls, the chanting, praying and invocation, digging. Here we were, in a place that was populated and public, a tourist picnic area along the highway. Our ceremony would be quite a spectacle to the casual observer. But again, once we began we were alone. The constant flow of tourists ceased for that short period of time. As soon as we finished, life resumed and there were many people.

After opening the Stargate I asked Jim to collect some water from the river. He headed down to the bank and began to play with the logs that had created a jam. With a larger log he tried to release the logs and open the jam. He finally freed the big log holding the water back and opened the flow. He then threw the log he had used as his tool into the river and the two logs flowed side by side, like partners in marriage, as one, down the river for as far as we could see. It was a very symbolic moment. Here we had just opened the Stargate merging shadow with Light. We opened this artery of water freeing mankind of all obstruction so all could flow easily back into the heart of the Mother. Jim had unblocked the *Heart of the Golden Rose* freeing all blockages. Heart of the Monster had become the *Heart of the Golden Rose,* now open to synthesize and transmute. Ceremony complete!

Opening the Stargates follows a precise sequence. The first three Stargates released and cleared any misqualified energy, laid a new blueprint for the new vibrational frequency, and stabilized the field in order that we could open the fourth Stargate. The fourth Stargate, *Heart of the Golden Rose* can be compared to the fourth dimension which serves as a portal or passageway bridging the third and fifth dimensions. Once activated, the *Heart of the Golden Rose* serves as a bridge between the first three Stargates and Stargates five, six and seven. Until this bridge was activated we would be unable to go on. "Merrily, merrily, merrily, merrily life is but a dream."

This fourth Stargate was much easier to find. We had been told that after opening *Swallows Window* there would be no more block between our inter-dimensional selves, that from then on there would be no doubt. No place for error. This was proving to be true. Each time we open one of the Stargates, the name comes to us, given to us from the higher realms reflecting the Stargate's vibration. Without thinking it just comes and thus the Stargate is christened. Upon activation a new energy emanates distinctly different from its historical landmark designation. Thus, Heart of the Monster became *Heart of the Golden Rose.* The circular rosebush pointed the way to this Stargate, the opening of the Golden Ray of Melchizedek.

I always like to be treated after we open a Stargate, rewarded with a special rock, a feather or a souvenir. I'm big on receiving presents. So after completing the opening of the *Heart of the Golden Rose* and as we were driving down the road, I asked Jim, "Are you going to buy me a treat?" Jim pointed out a smoke shop, not my kind of place; I wasn't interested in stopping there. Jim reminded me, however, that this was not Rancho Bernardo and we couldn't judge a book by its cover. Always so astute he is—the guide of all guides. I relented and said, "Okay, let's turn around." The air smelled of stale tobacco, wall to wall cigarettes interspersed with dusty, tacky, knickknacks. The clerk was wizened and old, skinny and wrinkled. I couldn't get out of there fast enough. But as we were leaving a small display case next to the cash register caught my eye. I didn't see it upon entering because it was blocked by the store clerk. It contained some Indian crafts. Nothing much, a few dusty pieces that must have been there for years, left by someone on consignment and forgotten. I noticed a small piece of beadwork with a rose on it. Interesting, but not exciting. It didn't call to me. Next to it was a medallion necklace and two matching earrings, finely beaded in a circle with small amethyst, onyx and white pearl seed beads. In the center was a brass (golden) heart. Two brass feathers hung at the base and two bells. Jim said I had to have it. "Oh no, it's $85, too expensive" I thought. Jim plopped down $100 and the necklace and earrings were in the bag and we were out the door before I knew it. The necklace found its home around Jim's neck and he has been wearing it ever since. It is the most amazing talisman. No coincidence how the *Heart of the Golden Rose* showed up as Jim's talisman.

A personal gift awaited us at Camas Prairie, a blessed ground of thanksgiving to the Nez Perce. Miles and miles of green prairie grass waved in the wind, a sea of peaceful green. It was a place of great sacrament where the Nez Perce through prayer, offerings and gratitude would give back to Mother Earth the abundance she gave. It is a prosperity site. We found a simple place off to the side of the road, no place in particular for the expanse was endless. We gave thanks for all the prosperity with which we have been blessed and the prosperity to come. With our simple thanks we merged our energy with the prayers of our Nez Perce brothers and sisters grateful for the limitless supply symbolized by the endless fields of grain. This was the time to reclaim our prosperity in all time and every dimension, past and future.

On to Tolo Lake, an ancient council site of the Nez Perce known as Tepehlewam. On June 8, 1877 the families of the different bands of Nez Perce had joined together at this annual camping ground for a celebration of music, games, horse racing and shared meals. It would be the final gathering where the tribal leaders of each band would meet in council to decide how to respond to the cavalry's demand to move off from their homeland. Although it was traditionally a gathering for celebration, this year an undercurrent of unrest and bitterness marred the festivities. Ultimately, a thoughtless insult by a young maiden to a proud young brave named Wahlitits started the chain of events that resulted in the White Bird Battle and led to the Nez Perce surrender four months later on October 5th.

Two years earlier in 1875, Tipyahlanah Siskan (Eagle Robe) had been attacked by white settlers. In the trial that followed the attackers were acquitted. On his deathbed Eagle Robe made his son, Wahlitits promise not to seek retribution. Now at the Tolo Lake gathering, in an off-hand comment, one of the women provoked Wahlitits by calling him a coward for not revenging his father's death. This was more than he could bear so with his cousin and nephew he left the celebration. They formed a raiding party and on the night of June 13th they left camp on the rising tide of emotion ultimately killing four settlers before their return. More raiding parties were formed and the long-held resentment for the suffering Nimiipuu at the hands of the white men had been unleashed. The cavalry responded and the Battle of White Bird began. The result was victory for the Nez Perce—thirty-four soldiers killed, only three Nez Perce slightly wounded. It was a hollow victory for the Nimiipuu however; it sealed their fate 1,100 miles later. As destiny would have it, Chief Joseph was away from camp caring for his wife when the tide of emotion swelled to violence. What was started in his absence was now his destiny to fulfill four months later. *"Hear me my chiefs, I am tired; my heart is sick and sad. From where the sun now stands I will fight no more. Forever."*

Tolo Lake holds the original vision of the Nez Perce people encoded in their sacred lineage by the Pleiadian Emissaries of Light 10,000 years ago. It was here Chief Joseph would appear throughout his many incarnations until the time in 1877 when the final council was held before the exodus of the Nez Perce. I was told this is a place where I would connect to Chief Joseph's vision.

Tolo Lake is part of the ancient planetary migration routes. It is a meridian in the energy grid system of Mother Gaia connecting Earth to all dimensions. In ancient times, highly evolved spiritual beings would teleport to this Tolo Lake from global sacred sites such as Stonehenge, the Himalayas, Mount Shasta and Machu Pichu. Like our modern day G-8, and now G-20 summits, world leaders would meet with their peers and gather in council and ceremony. It was the meeting point of many planetary and star nations, the galactic forerunner to the United Nations. For some reason this portal had shut down and we were here to open it.

Tolo Lake is ancient; wooly mammoths roamed here freely. Today it is a remnant of the lake it once was. It resembles a large pond, unique in that it is perfectly spherical. Its perimeter is surrounded by large volcanic boulders. These rocks are nowhere else to be found in the surrounding countryside. We had learned from Robin how to read the landscape. Anytime we spot an abrupt change in geology, or a place where no vegetation grows, or two dissimilar species growing side by side, "take note." This is a sign of an anomaly in the land, an energy shift, perhaps a sacred site? Today Tolo Lake is uninviting—dry, dusty, snake country. The sun is too bright, the landscape too stark, no vegetation, the water muddy. Not the Ritz Carlton one would think of for the gathering of elite world leaders of ancient times.

We were welcomed by an old fisherman in the parking lot warning us to watch out for snakes. "Really?" I gulped. "Is the Pope Catholic?" he retorted. "They come out at noon." It was 11:56 A.M. and with that he left us to ponder an unwanted encounter with scaly reptiles. We headed to the dock, my snake alert heightened and my spirit of adventure dampened. No way was I going into the scorched Earth to scurry among the snakes. We would open this portal from the dock. And so we did.

A dragonfly greeted us. Among other things the dragonfly signifies that magic and mystery are awakening for us. He tells us not to be too rational about anything. We are about to open a teleportation site. Through our third dimensional eyes we can't get more irrational! We hear the cow bird off in the distance. We're fond of and familiar with the cow bird from our morning walks along Lake Hodges in San Diego. We're not sure if he's a bird or a frog for we've never seen him, but he moos like a cow so we warmly call him the cow bird. There are geese flying off to the North and the pleasant song of the meadowlark brings some life to this stark landscape.

This ceremony would be different from the others. We were here to re-ignite the Ascension Keys. One by one we took each Key, spoke a prayer and playfully flicked each Key card into the lake. A child's game—God's children playing with God. Each symbol floated peacefully, some right side up, some upside down. In a procession we watched them one by one until they sank to their resting place. After opening this forgotten portal Jim wittily nicknamed the site Tolo Portal. "And now we Tolo Portal" became Jim's new favorite saying as we Journey OM.

The dry, hot, dusty, barren land at Tolo Lake was nothing compared to what we would encounter at our next stop, White Bird. Journey OM had suddenly reverted to third dimension Journey On.

It wasn't part of our plan, but after meeting with Robin, the Forest Service guide in Kamiah, we were compelled to go to White Bird. He described it as a place of rolling knolls, many mounds of hills where important people and things had been left. What he didn't tell us (and what we soon came to find out) is that the people and things which had "been left" were victims of sacrificial ritual. Perhaps there was something left for us to retrieve as there had been at other stops along the way? After all, this was the pathway leading up to the battlefield at White Bird.

When we arrived at White Bird the energy took our breath away—not in a good way. It was as if a vacuum had sucked it out of us. The air was hot; plains in the middle of nowhere were dusty and stifling dry. Every place we had gone before held wildflowers and prairie grass. Here, without a source of water, the prairie grass was burnt and scorched—the true trail of tears. No vegetation, tumbleweeds blowing. It was 83° but felt like 110°.

We started walking and immediately felt the oppression of the area. We were there to allow the souls an opportunity to forgive their oppressors and forgive themselves, to let these self-imposed captives know they could leave the imprisonment of the knolls and come back to Oneness. We sensed they were staying because they thought they were protected here and were fearful of being released. We chanted, prayed, offered sacred leaf and cornmeal so they would know that when they chose to free themselves they would be provided for, that there would be plenty—always. We explained to them their safety here was only an illusion, an untruth about their status in these deathly knolls.

As we walked on, it felt like a march, a funeral procession. We kept going. At the top of the hill there was one lone tree, nothing else around, the only tree in the area for miles. We were told by Robin we would see this tree and that it was centuries old, at least 2,000 years. It looked it. It was alive, but not healthy. We walked to the base of the tree to give thanks and ceremony. We took out the Ascension Keys *Love* and *Forgiveness* and buried them under a rock at the base of the tree. We nourished the tree with Peace Waters and thanked it for guarding these souls all these centuries.

As we headed up the hill further, I stopped. I was spent. It was difficult energy. There was no presence of angels. It felt like the life breath had been taken away. The souls *still* did not want to be released; they were *still* more comfortable being in their delusion than to be free. So we told them how beautiful it was. We shared with them what life was like "on the outside" and how happy we would be to have them join us.

On our way down the hill I had to sing. Had to! It was my method of protection. I sang and sang and sang. Childish songs…"Wake up, wake up you sleepy heads, get up, get up, get out of bed. Get your souls out of those knolls." "Two little blackbirds sitting on the hill, one named Jack, the other named Jill. Fly away Jack, fly away Jill." It was my shield, a guard to keep these entities from attaching to me. I could feel that once they had awakened they mistakenly thought they had to be with me. We just kept telling them it was okay, it was okay, and kept moving.

A few hours later I became ill, experiencing an immediate onset of sickness for no reason. I felt perfectly fine and then *wham!* Somehow I had not fully protected myself. The energy from Souls Knolls penetrated my physical being. There are "practitioners" who do this type of work; they hold contracts to help transmute energy of this sort. Not me! The sickness was a way to purge much of this energy. Or possibly I was still holding some of these soul fragments of my own and it was time to let them go. I was ill for twelve hours. Thanks to my reading of Joshua David Stone's books I knew of the Arcturian healing masters. I surrendered my condition to them to help me release anything I may have picked up along the way. I told them if God wanted me to continue on this journey my physical body had to be able to function because I was ready to stop.

It was the meeting with Robin that took us to Souls Knolls. It was unlike anything we experienced before, on the journey, or after. The Stargate Pilgrimage was one of joy, Love, frolicking in the higher frequencies of creation. This was just the opposite. It was the Broken Sequence. I was continually troubled by the incident at Souls Knolls so after the pilgrimage, after I arrived home, I sought understanding through channeling with Ahriah. This is what I learned:

We will say your going to this place at White Bird was directed by a lower aspect of yourself that was still challenging your own knowingness. Your first response, and we should tell you this for the future, is always the most accurate. To second guess yourself whether to meet Robin or not was to bring you back into a level of deception. For this one, Robin, truly wanted to investigate your holiness and do a form of sabotage against your body. He fully knew what that place which you call Souls Knolls would do to your energy. The tiredness you are feeling is still some of the aspects of those beings. Do you see? This is why we are telling you to cooperate fully with those who are ready to say "Yes." To move into a burial ground where many are not saying yes will distort the higher frequencies within you. For they want to pull you into that form of desecrated energy that is holding them in bondage.

I asked, "So was there any benefit accomplished? Or just a hard earned lesson for me?"

There were souls that were released; we would not tell you otherwise. There were those who did say yes. But the confrontation to your own Light system was too deeply dispersed for us to believe that it was the highest action to take. We would not reprimand you ever, for learning in a vortex of Light and shadow, but at this point in your ascension process we would ask you to follow the highest intention and not move yourself into that deep of toxicity. Those who are called to that work are called to it specifically because of their karma. It is not yours.

I learned even more of this cursed area of Earth from Judith:

Even before the conquest there were beings on this continent called the man eaters. They were possessed by the energy of what we call the dark forces. They were cruel beings, beyond imagination. They did not have hearts; they were called heartless beings.

The wounds and scars of Mother Earth go back to the time of the man eaters; back to the time they would conduct ceremonies and rituals. The souls in those knolls were killed and sacrificed and put there by the man eaters. Those were graves holding spirits that held the energy of torment and suffering that held the curse on the land. The Earth was cursed. That curse was set by the man eaters in ancient times before the conquest. You were on cursed land. It is this same spirit that possessed the man eaters that possesses the people disillusioned by supremacy today. From that curse came the possession that is supporting the psychosis of this belief of supremacy there. It was truly a demonic force that settled in the land of the Earth there.

People, unsuspecting people, who traveled through there would become afflicted because those attachments would travel with them. When you got so sick after being at Souls Knolls you were transmuting this demonic force. This was really a deep heart and soul part of your work. The work that you did there was releasing the ancient bondage of the Earth. You were channeling Light from the Pleiades and the Galactic Councils of Light were channeling Light through the Stargates into this cursed place. You were like the lady on the bow of the boat and the ship was "God-Ship."

I can see an energy line going like a beautiful golden serpent from each of those Stargates into the cursed land. And then spiraling and opening up the vibration of the Earth. The Earth was basically damned. It wasn't just a matter of the souls.

When they were released to the Light the liquid Light flowed through the Stargates into the cursed land and by the time you got there you had enough force behind you from opening the first four Stargates that you were capable of healing this land but it took a lot from your body. You were the medium.

There are satanic rituals being done in this dead zone. This area is being used for rituals. It can't be used anymore. The souls are free, the matrix has shifted. The souls that were released will go on about whatever they need to do to grow spiritually. It was a lock on the white supremacy nation. This curse is connected to everything that is happening in that area.

This revelation was most sobering to me and I knew in my heart this was true. There was no denying the feeling while we were at Souls Knolls or during the onset of my illness. What I experienced was the darkest of the dark, a place I had never been in this lifetime and would ask to never go again. I understood this "one time" wasn't a diversion; it was a very important part of my work and indeed, I must occasionally be able to go into those energies which are afflicting the people. All the same, I plead "Please don't ask me to do that again!" Yes, I was in the thick of it. The battlefield was White Bird and I would explain it as killing the dove, the bird of Peace.

I actually felt compassion for Robin. No judgment. I wanted to afford him a simple form of kindness. A good man being forced to act beyond his will. It is the power of the Love of Christ which changes the heart of the beast. The Christ Love. Hopefully, the gift of mirroring that Christ presence, of me seeing him in a different Light will allow Robin to see himself differently and break the shackles of his heart. It felt joyous to be a disciple of my Master, Lord Sananda. The Battlefield at White Bird was the point at which the full transformational aspects of our journey sunk in. I now realized it to be the heart of my work and that this full awakening could not have been accomplished until after the 4th Stargate, *Heart of the Golden Rose* had been opened, bringing shadow and Light into complete integration, into Oneness again.

We were tired. It was still Tuesday, but it felt like days had passed since waking up in Kamiah. The day's journey had been dusty and dry. Hot. The opening of the portals and the releasing accomplished at Tolo Portal and Souls Knolls were heavy lifting, tough work. It wasn't joyful. The angels didn't appear to be around much, as if to say, "Okay, you guys just take care of this and we'll catch up with you later!" The angels are much clearer about what is God and what is not. They would have no part of where we had been; they only hang out where joy, Love, pure Light and Peace surround. That's where you will find them.

We were headed to Weis Rockshelter where 8,000 years ago humans first made their home. This is the heart of the Mother, a shelter for her children. *"Here we will rest in the seed source knowledge that you are protected, guided and gifted."* After what we had just experienced at Souls Knolls these were welcome words, words given to me weeks ago. How did our guides know just what we needed to hear at just the right moment in order to continue on? This next Stargate is the Divine Mother coming to her children. It is the blending of the Love of Lady Nada and the Wisdom of Sophia. It carries the vibration of the dolphin codes and the cosmic blue Ray. The activation tone is "nnnnnn" of the first syllable in Waneen. The chakra is, of course, the heart chakra.

Ascended Master Lady Nada is chohan of the Sixth Ray, the ruby and gold Ray of Peace, brotherhood and service to mankind. She is the essence of pure Love expressed through service to life. On Atlantis Nada was a priestess in the Temple of Love. In her final incarnation 2,700 years ago, Nada was the youngest of a large family of exceptionally gifted children. Oftentimes ignored and belittled, she struggled to be accepted by her family. Archangel Chamuel appeared to her and taught her how to draw God's Love from the flame in her heart and to radiate it into the hearts of her sisters, increasing their musical abilities so they might bless others and uplift humanity's culture through the arts. Her gift to her family went unrecognized; a selfless gift of Love for the benefit of her sisters and the cultural arts. She is the twin flame of Lord Sananda. Sophia is the Goddess of Wisdom. She lives in all women and her strength and grace inspire and give knowledge in the ways of nurturing. Sophia is the Celestial Mother and the Spirit of God uniting Father and Child.

We were envisioning a babbling brook where we could sit and maybe even lay down for a while. With that desire in mind we followed the signs to Weis Rockshelter along a seven mile country road. Soon after leaving the highway we dropped into a canyon. Huge granite walls towered on each side of the narrow passageway. It was like entering the birth canal, entering the womb. The atmosphere changed from dry and hot to moist and cool. The bright glaring sun transformed to dappled sunlight. It felt so good our souls began singing. Since we didn't know where we would end up we relished the feelings of being immersed in this nurturing place.

We noted that at every Stargate there would be a Keeper; that once we discovered the gateway and passed through we could be sure the Stargate was nearby. Finding each Stargate was always a treasure hunt. The Stargate Keeper, our animal guide, would lead us to the ceremony, and oftentimes, animals, birds and insects from the previous Stargates would join the festivities. The gateway to *Peace Waters* was obvious. The granite walls opened up to a grassy incline where to the left was a large outcropping. Jim saw it immediately, a stone sculpture up on the hill. That's why he's the Scout. Me, I just wander in oblivion. Jim is much more attuned to reading the clues. He described the rock outcropping as a talking figurine, both human and animal with its mouth open screaming at a perched cat above. For what seemed like eternity he kept trying to get me to see the rock formation through his eyes. The harder I tried the more obscure it became. Finally I saw a cat, sphinx-like with a baby on his back. Not the image Jim was seeing, but at least I was seeing something. Restless and frustrated, still carrying the fatigue of the Souls Knolls I impatiently said, "Okay, we know it's the gate. Take a picture and you can show me on the computer." We both agreed it was the guardian entrance to heart of the Mother, Stargate #5—*Peace Waters.*

We later learned the stone sculpture, similar to the creation of crop circles and the rock tailings at *Swallows Window,* is the work of the Pleiadians. The Pleiadians are teaching us and giving us tools through the use of Earth's formations—water, stone and plant life. These visions are impregnated and held into Mother Earth. Once materialized the energies descend into the vortex and act like an acupressure point for access by Light Workers who are assisting in the ascension process. This is about Law, the new Law of resurrection and ascension. This land called Weis Rockshelter, home to the Nez Perce thousands of years ago carried the Divine codes of Love and Peace. For thousands of years the Nez Perce carried these encodements until eons later when the codes would be activated for Chief Joseph to choose Peace over war in 1877. Now once again these codes of Peace and Love are being returned to all of us.

Pictures taken, we gave the sculpture a quick thank you for leading the way and showing us the entrance key. Our awareness heightened and in search of the location of the Stargate, we slowed down and stopped at the historical landmark Weis

Rockshelter, a system of caves under a huge granite overhang where humans lived for 8,000 years. We could see why. It was prime real estate. The caves were beautiful, but now inaccessible. They had been backfilled as preservation from damage and to keep people out. As we neared the caves we could tell that those not filled with dirt were guarded naturally by huge brambles armed with inch-long thorns. They looked centuries old. They were impenetrable. There was no getting by. We gave another thanks to the caves, but knew it wasn't the place of the Stargate so we journeyed on.

Jim took off exploring across the country road, down a small incline to find a soft babbling creek, precisely what we had dreamed of many miles back. He was searching for a safe crossing. The stream wasn't too big and by moving a few stones, although wet and mossy, he easily created a stepping stone bridge. He tiptoed across his newly created passage and found the perfect walking stick as an aid for me. While he was scouting about I remained at the car collecting all of our supplies and preparing to open the Stargate.

As soon as we crossed the stream we laid down our prayer mat and took off our shoes and socks. The small opening was covered in thigh high grass reeds. Jim had stomped them down to create a place to sit and in so doing, created a reed mat we could stand on in the shallow water. It was Divine, the water cooling, but not cold. Throughout our journey we've been following rivers and streams; being spring in the mountains, the water is frigid (six seconds is all we could stand the last time we braved the current). The runoff is laden with silt and most rivers and streams are raging this time of year, too swift for safe entry. This stream was peaceful, unlike anything we had encountered. There was no question this was the Stargate we were meant to find.

We refreshed and rejuvenated in the flowing waters, surrendering all we had done previously. It had been a long day, starting at Pebble Beach, breakfast with Robin, opening *Heart of the Golden Rose,* thanksgiving at Camas Prairie, re-opening Tolo Portal and releasing the curse on the land and the captive souls at Souls Knolls. Opening two Stargates in one day was a lot as we had realized on our first day opening *Dolphin's Halo* and *Ancient Wisdom.* This was beyond our endurance—we were only able to accomplish what we did through the Grace of God. He had a mission for us and all was provided for, including unlimited energy.

We were now ready for ceremony. Among other things we blessed the creek with Lady of Lourdes holy water and Peace Waters connecting to the heart of the Mother from around the world. As I read the invocation prayer I could hear in the distance the sound of someone with their radio. Or was it someone talking? The "talking" stopped me mid-sentence several times; I would look up to see if anyone was nearby picnicking. We were miles off the main two lane road in a very isolated area, but it sounded very real. Jim noticed it too, although neither one of us mentioned it to the other until after the ceremony. "Did you hear that?" "Yeah!" "Did you hear that?" "Yeah!" It turned out to be the babbling brook. It was talking to us! Speaking a language we knew, but didn't know. It was literally out of this world, the manner in which the inner middle Earth beings speak. They send the language from middle Earth through the waterways. The cliché "babbling brook" is exactly that—the expression of energy and communication from middle Earth beings. There are many elementals, devas, what we think of as trolls and elves, many of the Earth workers who hold themselves under Earth and speak through the waterways. They were singing us on our way, singing in joyful abandonment to our calling, blessing us with their chanting. A new group of beings had joined the party. Along with the animals, birds and insects our new Middle Earth friends jumped into the assemblage. The swallows were there to assist us and like the robins, once they joined the journey they didn't want to leave. They had been with us at every stop since the opening of *Swallows Window* on Monday.

This journey is similarly a "tiptoe through the garden." At every stop Jim would discreetly wander away to return with a wildflower. He'd pull it out from behind his back and with great surprise I'd *ooh* and *ahh,* never tiring of delighting in this simple act of Love, small gestures taking on magnificence beyond their kindness. I have carefully preserved each of them.

What a day! But we weren't finished. With any luck we could drive another four hours in daylight and make it across Lolo Pass to arrive in Missoula, Montana by midnight. We had been so immersed in the higher planes we were ready to kick back and ground ourselves in some good old country music. Off we go. With my feet on the dashboard, Alan Jackson on the CD and singing along to our favorite songs we traveled on down the road, carefree, unaware of our speed, not a car in sight on this stretch of two lane road. Out of nowhere lights flashed behind us—ugh!—the sheriff.

Jim pulled over and a young man with a badge, younger than our son, began his interrogation. "Do you know how fast you were going?" "Didn't you see me?" "Do you have any weapons in the car?" Weapons in the car? Question after question. Not wanting to sound disrespectful, we didn't know how to answer. We looked a sight! Jim hadn't shaved since Saturday. We were dusty and dirty and around his neck Jim was wearing the big Golden Heart Medallion. Our looks alone rendered us questionable. The sheriff collected our paperwork, called us in and returned with a ticket. "Giving you a break," he said. "You were clocked at 73 mph. Seventy miles is $75; over that $120." So much for my "God calling" and not being at the affect of the lower dimensional occurrences such as speeding tickets! Lesson learned—being obstructed will never be fully negated from my life as I go about this work. The Masters can protect me, but there are still instances where beings of a lower vibration will see the road I am on and become an obstruction. I will continue to be tested. The officer could feel the Light and Love in the car and tried to obstruct it as did the ranger, Robin.

Crossing Lolo Pass in the day takes concentration. It's a winding two lane road, with high granite walls to the left and steep canyon drops to the river below. There are guardrails, but not ones you would ever want to put to the test. Installed at the time the highway was built they have long lost their purpose. It's breathtaking to view and breath-holding to drive. Driving at night makes it all the more treacherous. Normally Jim would be antsy stuck behind three semi-trucks, but this night they were a gift, our deer scouts. Anyone who has driven the roads of the West has encountered deer leaping unexpectedly into their path. It's a common site to see broken windshields and crumpled front ends. It happens so frequently some don't even bother with the repairs—the semis were a welcome shield.

We try to limit our days from sunrise to sunset. A summer day this far north is a fifteen hour day. We were between stopping places with nowhere to go and had another full day of driving—four hundred miles tomorrow through Montana into Wyoming—so we journeyed on to spend the night in Missoula. A pattern has emerged, one I'm not proud to confess. Every evening when our day's assignment has been achieved, I am exhausted and ready to give up. But Jim, the incredible guide and guardian, always responds with encouragement. "Let's see how we feel in the morning." Tonight was no different. Once we get to Missoula (I'm thinking to myself) we'd only be three hours away from Whitefish. We could break the pilgrimage up into stages and complete the Stargate openings over the next few months. I was sick from the experience at Souls Knolls and ready to go home.

Near the top of the pass we came upon wreckage. A semi had gone off the road and not too long ago. One lane was still closed, multiple tow trucks trying to figure out how to remove the wreckage. The injured had already been transferred, only the metal, steel and glass remained. We were sobered by the sight. This journey was not without its dangers. Divine timing we thought. Had we received a gift in disguise a few hours earlier? Had we not been stopped by the sheriff in Idaho would we have been at this exact spot at the time of the accident? Now the speeding ticket seemed like a small price to pay for what could have been ahead.

We arrived in Missoula at midnight—exhausted. I had been getting steadily sicker, wounded from Souls Knolls. First stop, a grocery store for over the counter remedies to get me through the night. How readily I give up my holistic ways in the face of discomfort! The manager was just locking up but waved us in, turned the lights back on and assisted with our goods—another helper from Above. We were looking forward to our night in Missoula, the "big city" after wilderness. We had lived in Missoula in the early 80s with our baby son and had fond memories of the University of Montana and our life there. Tomorrow was Jim's birthday so we planned to splurge—a room with a view of the Clark Fork, sleeping to the sound of the rushing river. Not meant to be. What a disappointment! It was worn and shabby and freezing cold. We tossed and turned—me sick, Jim tired—thankful for sunrise so we could get up.

Broken Sequence
0
1 Kilometer
0
1 Mile
North
East
Knoll
West
Knoll
Trail
You Are Here

Missoula
Greenough
Bonner
Lolo
Lolo Hot Sprs.
Drummond
Headquarters
Stevensville
Maxville
Philipsburg
Corvallis
Lowell
Grangeville
Darby
Conner
CONTINENTAL DIVIDE
Big Hole Nat'l Battlefield
Wisdom
Elk City
Golden
White Bird
Lucile
North Fork
Shoup
Jackson
Warren
Burgdorf
Cobalt
Yellow Pine
Salmon
Tendoy
Grant
Leadore
Dell
Lima
Lakeview
Humphrey
May
Patterson
Challis
Clayton
Spencer
Dubois
Ashton
Marysville
St. Anthony
Smiths Ferry
Banks
Lowman
Sawtooth Nat'l Rec. Area
Hamer
Teton
Rexburg
Tetonia
Mackay
Horseshoe Bend
Atlanta
Howe
Mud Lake
Menan
Roberts
Old Faithful
Mammoth Hot Springs
Grand Teton Nat'l Park

Wednesday, May 27, 2009

Yesterday's illness and the late night drive across Lolo Pass in the dark really challenged both of us. And yet we woke up this morning feeling engaged and alive and ready to carry on. So with Starbucks in hand we head down the road: Missoula to Yellowstone Park down to Jenny Lake to Stargate #6. Starbucks to Stargates! The day seemed easy—steady driving with no stops and starts, a rhythm where time and miles flowed. Timeless, we enjoy the quiet company of each other. No maps to read, instructions to follow, smooth sailing on our way to Jenny Lake from Missoula. The Interstate felt great after dirt roads, two lane highways and twisty-twining curves through ravines and canyons. We arrived in Livingston by noon then headed south to Gardiner, the north entrance to Yellowstone Park.

So far we had been eating very healthily. Jim had prepared two coolers of meals and snacks, hummus, pita, olives, tomatoes, fresh vegetables, crackers and lefse—everything for cellular nutrition. But by day five we were tiring of eating the same fare and thought we'd venture off the beaten path to restaurant dining. In Gardiner we stopped the beer delivery guy in the middle of the street, figuring he would know all the great places to get a good bite. "Where's a good place for French fries, and maybe a veggie burger?" We had been craving fries since Sunday night in Kamiah. "Don't know 'bout veggie burgers, but the K-Bar has a great cook and great fries." That's all we needed for the continuation of "Fry Happy."

The K-Bar was a classic western style bar, the kind I frequented in my early twenties growing up in Montana. This one, however, was clean and absent the stale beer and cigarette smell (either enlightenment or intolerance). Dottie, a cute five foot fifty year old with lots of spunk, ran the bar and took the orders. Besides us, there were a few locals and a couple of tourists on their way to the Park. It was easy to carry on conversations amongst one another and the place became lively. To our surprise they had a black bean vegetarian burger on the menu! We ordered two with all the works and fries. The best black bean veggie burgers and French fries we've ever had. We had found burger heaven in Gardiner at the K-Bar.

As we entered Yellowstone Park we paradoxically felt the absence of life. Here in a national sanctuary where wildlife is abundant and animals roam freely, the constant barrage of tourists had caused the animals to retreat. In a sense they were there in physical form, but their spirits were veiled. It reminded me of what we do to each other when we don't honor our boundaries or don't allow each other to express who we are, freely without threat or harm. It was the same lesson the evolved spirits living in Aneroid Peak of the Wallowa Mountains taught us by their reluctance to show themselves. Our prejudice, our unwillingness to open to "anything's possible," clinging to what doesn't fit our reality, stifles us.

There weren't too many tourists yet; it was early in the season, but the energy had clearly shifted. For five days we had traveled in some of the most beautiful, pristine areas of Creation. The veils were thin. It was easy to commune with the animals, the mineral kingdom, the plants and the waterways. Here in Yellowstone, while beautiful, it had obviously been affected by the many people passing through. We could feel the barriers and the baggage the tourists had left behind. Nature was forced to conceal her secrets and her guard was up. I tried to break through. "Hey, it's us. Show us your splendor." But all remained hidden except for the small herd of bison not seeming to care. Off in the distance a few other residents, elk and big horn sheep with newborn observed us, but they didn't greet us like we had become accustomed. They kept to themselves. The bison in particular were quite impressive—serene and sweet in their hugeness—simply caring for their young. Shedding their winter coats they looked a bit tattered. As cars pulled over to gawk, I could imagine the buffalo saying under their breath, "What are you looking at? Take a picture it will last longer!"

There are Light Workers focused on this sacred land in Yellowstone Park, helping to pacify the elementals, soothing their anger for humankind's disrespect over eons of time, hoping to keep the volatile cauldrons beneath the surface from exploding. I expressed my gratitude to them for taking on this responsibility and passed through the entrance gate to the Tetons. We as humans easily forget we're not the only beings who occupy this beautiful planet. The elementals and angelic kingdom also call Mother Gaia their home.

We entered the Grand Teton National Park around 3:00 P.M. and another 20 miles down the road checked into the Jackson Lake Lodge to call it an early day. It was Jim's birthday after all, and it would be nice to celebrate. We had been going from dawn to dusk every day with a midnighter over Lolo Pass. God was keeping us energized and nourished, but it *is* a bit difficult for the physical body to keep up with God's pace. Our plan was to find a beautiful lodge, check in early, and make it a short pilgrimage day. Maybe even do some laundry (Jim's idea, not mine). We might get some evening scouting in, check out Jenny Lake and the environs in preparation for opening Stargate #6 first thing in the morning. Afterward, we would hit the road nonstop to Bear's Paw, a mere 400+ miles north from our present location. That was the plan. But as we learned on day one, God is the perfect travel planner and our plotting always falls short of His Divine Order.

Jackson Lake Lodge is a beautiful hotel. The main Lodge serves as the hub for check-in; there are shops, restaurants and panoramic views from floor to ceiling through windows three stories high. Room accommodations are scattered around the property condo-style. You pay for the view. The accommodations are sparse, probably designed so as not to take away from the majesty of the scenery. It feels like we've arrived on "opening day." Nothing's quite ready. The staff is young—students and travelers from all over the world paying their way to adventure by working at the Lodge. It's a wonderful lifestyle and the young adventurers are eager to please; they carry the sparks of fun and flexibility. They are a delight to be with and their enthusiasm makes up for their inexperience. The kinks are still being worked out from the winter closure. What unfolded over the next twelve hours was a comedy of errors. In the end all we could do was laugh. Fortunately, there was very little occupancy so we were not charged rack rate. In fact, after the manager heard of our many mishaps (broken glass on our patio, jammed windows, inoperative ice machine, entry doors blocked by furniture, dead smoke alarm battery constantly beeping, and a drain plugged up by grout from sloppy repair), he comped our room (after the credit card machine double charged us). Not necessary, but appreciated—a simple gift given.

Adjusting to the inspiring impact of the Tetons we settled in. I was especially excited to take a nap after five days on the road; Jim couldn't wait to get down the road to the campground's laundry services. It was a well-earned reprieve from our intense journeying, each of us doing "our thing." A few hours later we enjoyed the ambiance of a 50s style diner. All seating was counter style so we shared our meal with the few other tourists braving it in the early season. We enjoyed the time mingling with the French, the Japanese and the German—all speaking different languages but basically saying the same thing. It was slow so the Manager, with time on his hands and not much to do, made huckleberry shakes for everyone. The French were not impressed; they would have preferred strawberry!

Well-rested from my late afternoon nap, upon returning to our room I had work to do. We were committed to finding and opening every Stargate and this required detailed follow-up every step of the way. Not sure why, but knowing it was part of the process, I would journal at each interval. For the next few hours, papers spread across the bed I wrote, cut, pasted, taped and chronicled our pilgrimage. Jim kept records on the camera; me with my pen.

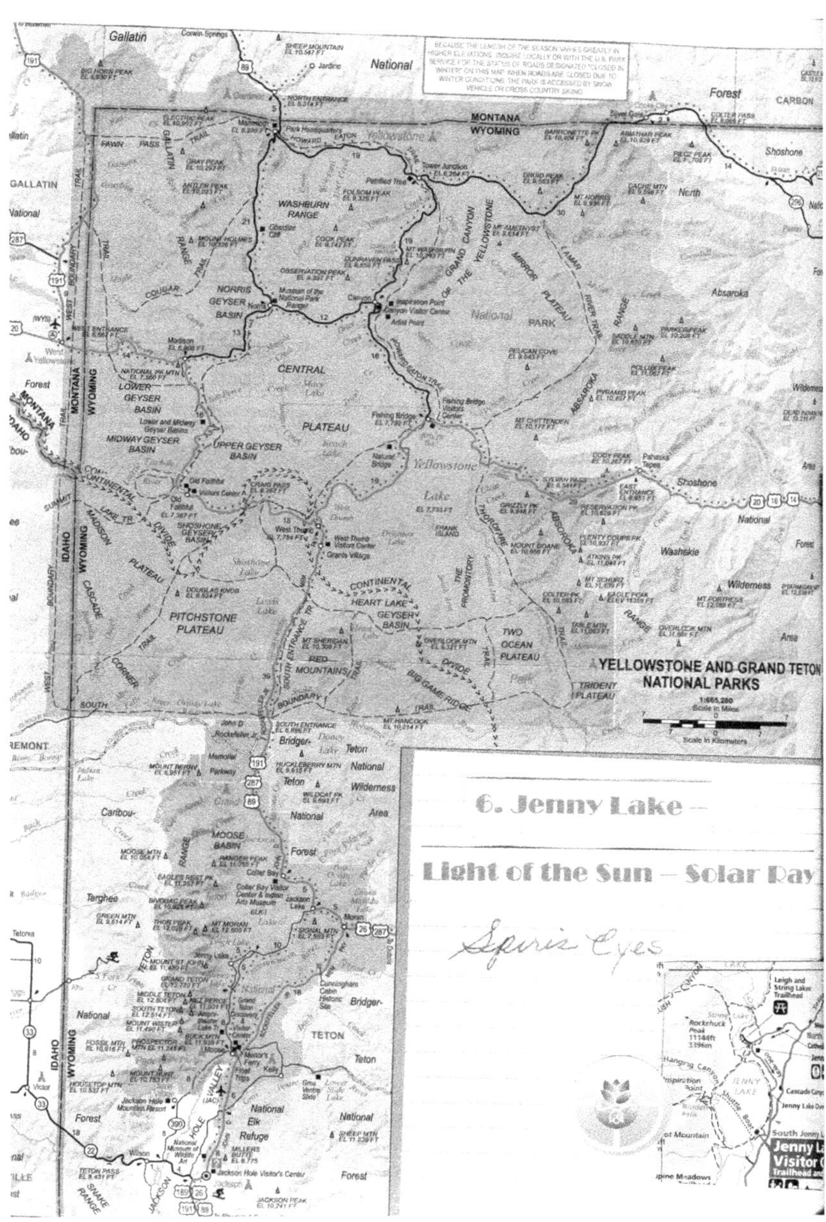
YELLOWSTONE AND GRAND TETON NATIONAL PARKS
6. Jenny Lake –
Light of the Sun – Solar Ray
Spiris Eyes
MONTANA
WYOMING
IDAHO
WASHBURN RANGE
NORRIS GEYSER BASIN
CENTRAL PLATEAU
LOWER GEYSER BASIN
MIDWAY GEYSER BASIN
UPPER GEYSER BASIN
Yellowstone Lake
PITCHSTONE PLATEAU
TWO OCEAN PLATEAU
RED MOUNTAINS
MIRROR PLATEAU
Absaroka
Shoshone
Gallatin
National
Forest
Teton Wilderness
Jenny Lake
Leigh and String Lakes Trailhead
Rockchuck Peak
Inspiration Point
South Jenny Lake
National Elk Refuge

Thursday, May 28, 2009

Good morning star shine! It's May 28th and we're at Jackson Lake Lodge. I opened my eyes and soul to the Grand Tetons, an astounding picture upon awakening. Is this a dream? My first sight was a cloud formation identical to the mountain peak. Every crevice, every ridge was outlined in the cloud. I knew immediately I was being shown the etheric retreat of the Ascended Masters. I had read of this astonishing inner plane retreat and now I was seeing a glimpse of its reality. I jostled Jim out of his sleep. "Quick, grab the camera! Look!" But in an instant it was gone, not to be revealed on film, much like the experience at Mount Aneroid in the Wallowas. The Ascended Masters were showing me their etheric home—As Above, So Below.

I hurried out of bed and set my gaze out the window facing east. The sky was on fire with the rising sun—luminous yellow, gold and orange, colors surreal to our natural eyes. This made perfect sense. No wonder. Today we are opening the Solar Ray, the Ray of Illumination. So amazingly perfect—always in Divine Order! The sixth Stargate is embraced by Lord Lanto and Lord Kuthumi. Lord Lanto's retreat is the Royal Teton Retreat in the Grand Teton Mountain Range. The Solar Ray holds the energy vibration of Wisdom and Knowledge; the expansion of Light through Illumination. It is the Ray of abundance and wealth, happiness, joy and Universal Christ Consciousness—that about covers it all!

The gifts of this Stargate are many. Like the Rays, once they are fully mastered they merge with each other and become one; the many gifts and virtues specific to one Ray become attainable from all the Sacred Rays. This also happens with the chakra system in the physical body. As we spiritually evolve, rather than the singular individualized chakras along the spine, an enlightened individual will have a single column of pure white Light. Makes sense—isn't white the essence of all color?

There were many gifts, many insights and numerous lessons waiting to be revealed. At the last Stargate, *Peace Waters,* we opened the Heart of the Divine Goddess. Here we would open the Mind of the Father. Now complete—Heart and Mind as One—the Divine Feminine and Divine Masculine as One. This is the Stargate where we and all of mankind will receive the bestowment of Divine Wisdom from Lord Lanto and Lord Kuthumi. Little did I know it was here that I would receive a gift—the integration of the 3rd eye with the physical eyes allowing me to see all dimensions through the physical eyes (a gift incidentally, available to us all).

We said good-bye to Jackson Lake Lodge and headed south. Stopping to bless the Snake River with Peace Waters from Whitefish we were greeted by swallows. We traveled down the road to the south of Jenny Lake until we came to a parking lot and the beginning of trailheads. It was early morning. It was radiant. The chill was in the air, low 40s but the sun was bright and we were ahead of the tourist parade. We chose the trail to Hidden Falls. I began singing to Lord Lanto to illumine the way, asking Lord Melchizedek to pinpoint the spot.

When we reached Jenny Lake it was perfectly still. The reflections of the mountains on the lake were a mirror image. We took pictures and seconds after we took the photos a breeze picked up creating ripples. Then a small boat stirred up the waters. In an instant the reflection was gone. Time tricks us humans. Living inter-dimensionally there is no time or space—visions of the mountains and lake reflecting each other would seem to last forever as long as our interest and attention were bringing us joy. But in an instant we can lose that high frequency focus and quickly and abruptly find ourselves landed back in third dimension where time does exist. And that's when those miracle moments disappear in a flash. The starship at *Swallows Window* and the cloud peak at Grand Teton are two examples of this phenomenon.

We had hiked only a short while, not very far when we came upon a large rock outcropping—the only one on the trail, pure white quartz. It didn't take us long to find the key to this Stargate. We knew immediately this was the Stargate Keeper, the guardian of the portal. But it happened so quickly. It's like me shopping. I can't buy the first thing I see even if it is the most perfect item. I have to continue shopping "just to be sure." So we spent some time exploring and scrambling around "just to be sure." Our bird friends, two wild geese honking, a hummingbird fluttering and robin chirping greeted our arrival, discordant but somehow harmonic.

Further from the lakeshore we met a mountain grouse. We had opened five Stargates and we had learned our lessons well. Another sign—no question he was our guide for this Stargate. He was happily eating, not bothered or concerned by us. If this was the job he was given—to direct us to the Stargate—he was clearly bored with it all. By now we consider ourselves Master Stargate Openers. How quickly we take the synchronicities and signs for granted. Hasn't it always been this way, this gift of trust, intuition and knowing? We've had it all along. God must be laughing with us as we remember who we truly are and we begin to reclaim our gifts.

The male grouse sent out his warning, clearing the way for the ceremony and Stargate opening to begin. We were undisturbed by tourists and hikers. Even though the late morning was bringing out the many travelers from their campsites, we were protected by the Masters for this sacred activation. Without question the quartz rock was the Stargate Keeper and Mr. Grouse was the greeter. The robin was nearby—our dear friend—the one connecting us on this soul journey, this star journey, every step of the way. It never ceased to amaze us.

We veer off trail and take a left up and across some logs, following the grouse who leads us to a meadow. The meadow, no bigger than our blanket, was encircled by pine trees with an opening directly to the Grand Teton Peak. Again womb-like; again a familiar landmark similar to *Dolphin's Halo* and *Ancient Wisdom*—rounds of pines, a circular meadow with direct view of a mountain peak. From the meadow we had a full view of Teton's base to its peak. This was the Stargate, no doubt, but just for fun, I took out the pendulum. Yes! It began swinging wildly. The meadow was illumined, dappled in sunlight, just enough to warm us, seemingly much warmer than the 40ish degrees the thermometer indicated. It felt like 70°. It was peaceful, the birds were singing and we knew this was the spot. The feminine womb and the masculine peak—the significance was not lost on us—the total mergence into Oneness. Thank you, Ascended Masters, Lord Lanto, Lord Melchizedek and Lord Kuthumi for showing us the way. The Grand Teton was shining in full splendor.

We took out our prayer blanket and sacred bundles, played the crystal bowls and set up for our special ceremony. As I began, I was startled by a rustling sound, like the starting of a lawn mower. Mr. Grouse was letting us know he was here. Initially I thought it was a bear. I stopped and asked permission from the animal kingdom to be here, to welcome us to this sacred space and to protect us. Most importantly, I asked, "Please do not make your presence known. We will only be here a short while." I promised. "And we'll leave it in pristine condition." Honoring our request the "big boys" (the bear, the moose, the mountain lion) left us to our intention and we were only graced with Mr. Grouse, hummingbird, robin and goose. We weren't far off the path, just a few hundred feet. You couldn't see us, but anyone nearby could clearly hear us. We're in a National Park, synonymous with lots of tourists and hikers. But again, as we had come to expect, all traffic stopped while we were reverently engaged.

We discovered later that Mr. Grouse was doing more than strutting his stuff. He was telling everyone else to steer clear and stay away. Jim took up his shield of the Ruby Knight and protectively walked the perimeter of the meadow. He could hear the snorting animal and thought it could be a bear. Thankfully, he didn't alert me. Come to find out, during our ceremony an elk stopped by, evidenced by fresh droppings on our return trip down the trail. Everybody wants to join the party!

There was an old log tree trunk close by and it was the place Jim selected to bury the bundle. We found another log similar to the old log and placed it over the Stargate site completing the activation. It was splendor! The towering mountain and the serene stillness of the meadow—it was the perfect spot. We were in a venerable state, overwhelmed by God and His Love. We couldn't move, mesmerized by the warmth, the Peace. It was a place of ecstasy, a cocoon of Eternal Love. We didn't want to leave the One Still Point—the Heart of the Mother and the Protection of God our Father. It was a place of majesty. We sat in the stillness.

I felt the desire to meditate. I packed up our things and sat back down to envelop the calm. I was unable to close my eyes. As soon as I would shut them, they would pop open and fix on the peak of the Grand Teton. I hear a message coming from within: *With these eyes I see. With these eyes I see.* What does that mean? All the enlightened beings and spiritual gurus I have met along the way see with the 3rd eye. Me? I could never see the colors, the beauty, the etheric visions they described. It has always troubled me. If I am on my ascension path, then why can't I see with my 3rd eye? I have spent countless sessions and thousands of dollars trying to clear whatever was obstructing my sightline to God.

I try to meditate on the words, but my eyes won't close and my mind gets in the way. *The Masters are visible and are always with you. With-in has merged with-out. It is all One and there is no longer any going 'within' without creating separation from the One.* Gradually, I awaken to the message. "With these eyes I see!" The 3rd eye has merged with the physical eyes. I know now that on a conscious level I see the Divine with these blue-green eyes—a gift of incredible proportion. I embrace being an enlightened individual. To say less, out of false humility or ego, would be to deny my God Presence and the revelations gifted me. This lifetime, with reverence and gratitude, I accept fully my Divinity, a birthright I rejected lifetime after lifetime. Realizing the 3rd eye and the physical eyes have merged into one, meditation is no longer a place of going within; it is actually a point of separation. I sat there in a state of suspended awe. Not "Aha!" but "Awe!" *With In* had merged *With Out*—there is no inside/outside. It is all God Presence.

And the sixth Stargate, *Spires Eyes,* was christened. Jim and I are encouraged by how easy opening the Stargates has become. At first it was difficult to determine the location. Even with all of the preparations and down loadings from the Pleiadian Emissaries of Light connecting to the geo-magnetic field and frequencies of the Earth, it still felt like trying to solve a calculus or physics problem. Twelve years of Catholic education bestowed excellent spelling and grammar skills—not so math or science. But hey, after six Stargate openings and lots of practice with the geo-magnetic fields (plus owning our power) we are gravitating directly to them.

That said, as we look around and comprehend the enormity of this land we are further humbled. How is it we can pinpoint the seemingly impossible spot? Even a few feet off and the pendulum says "No." The Stargate is exact. There is no doubt—it is truly a miracle. Opening *Spires Eyes* felt like opening the entrance to the Ascended Masters etheric retreat for all to come. Once *Spires Eyes* was open all of the Ascension Keys became available to mankind. The Ascended Masters' Light, their Vibration, their Wisdom, Knowledge and Guidance will easily flow through Earth and to humankind. Where before these keys were grounded in each of the geographic etheric temples, the energy now flows freely, connecting all of the sacred sites of Mother Gaia and the entire Universe. Personal access to communing with our Masters is more readily available than ever before.

This meadow and the soaring Teton peak remind me of the towering Canadian Rockies near Lake Louise where I visited Archangel Michael's etheric temple last summer. There's a similarity in these places. I learned later that Archangel Michael's feminine complement, Archangel Faith's etheric retreat is here at Jenny Lake. That's how I am feeling the connection. The veils, if not gone, are invisibly thin. I understand now there is more to come to this new calling and I will be visiting Lake Louise again soon to complete what I initiated last summer.

It was late morning by the time we completed the activation of *Spires Eyes.* Our journey had taken us to the southernmost point of our pilgrimage and we were on the return loop. One more Stargate to open 450 miles away, back through Wyoming, then north through Montana to Bear's Paw Mountain forty miles south of Canada. We have crisscrossed the fourth largest state in the United States, a land mass of 147,046 square miles in two days. Traveling through the

National Parks is slow going, but once traversed we'd be moving right along, hopefully arriving in Havre, Montana in time for a good night's rest. For now it's back to Gardiner where black bean veggie burgers and fries are on our mind. No need for menus—same as yesterday.

Thirty years ago, shortly after our wedding we took a "honey-moon" to Chico Hot Springs, a place nestled in the middle of nowhere, in the shadow of Emigrant Peak in Paradise Valley, Pray, Montana where the natural hot springs still flow. Not much has changed since the early 1900s or for that matter, since 1979 when we last visited. The hotel built in 1900 is eerily the same. A few upgrades here and there, nothing noticeable. The bar still draws a crowd in mid-afternoon and the famous sign: "Notice the "P" is missing from ool and we'd like to keep it that way" reminding visitors of pool etiquette is still posted. Jim got a chuckle back then and he chuckles now—another photo op. The only difference between 1979 and now is the license plates on the newer model autos and the fact that Chico Hot Springs has been discovered; it's no longer a "locals" hangout. We had a memorable soak, relaxed, very relaxed, maybe too relaxed to be driving after a big meal and hot waters. After buying a few postcards for our journal we begin the long trek to Chinook, Montana the site of Chief Joseph's surrender at Bear's Paw forty miles short of his freedom in Canada. How fitting of God to select Chico as my choice point—a place of personal history. I thought I was fully prepared for what was to come.

As I shared earlier, my life agreement as a walk-in of this soul body was complete; I had cleared her karma as agreed in my contract. It was written in the Akashic records. This was the moment I prayed for and waited for, most times impatiently. Here, finally was the time when I could leave this physical plane and return to the concept of what I thought of as "home." Now it was time—and I chose "No." Let me explain. During a channeling with Ahriah on May 20th prior to our departure I was given life-altering information. Lord Melchizedek told me that near the Stargate we were approaching I would encounter the pinnacle point. It would be the last integration, the full integration of the crown chakra and the illumination of the lotus. It would be a place where, in the future, many would choose to ascend having reached this pinnacle point in their own evolutions. I was told to be very clear when I was near this site to choose to stay in the physical body for I would be offered "opportunity."

So this was it, my point of choice to leave the planet. As my mind grasped the enormity of this choice my ego fought tooth and nail to survive. I tiptoed into fear and asked about Jim. "Will Jim be okay there?" I knew well enough I had not evolved nearly to the point to simply ascend, that while at this level of enlightenment, while still living in a physical body on Earth, a catalyst would be required to ascend, most probably an accident of some sort. Some would call this death. My friend Patrick and I have joked for many years about the "pink purse." There was an occurrence where a woman had ascended, simply lifting the body. No death. No body. Only her pink purse remained. Sounds magical, but it left many problems for those who remained behind, namely her husband and the incriminations that ensued in the search for the body. No, I would not want that for my beloved Jim.

Yes, Jim will be okay. Jim will not be affected because his intention as your protector is clear. He is not asking to go home. It is you who will have an opportunity.

Oh boy! For the past month I had been immersed in the planning and excitement of this pilgrimage. I had been blessed with incredible initiations and Light body activations. I was experiencing Heaven on Earth in its truest form. I had full awareness that life on Earth actually could be Heaven on Earth, that there is no "home" to go to. Once we find God within and assimilate our I AM Presence we are home—here, there, wherever I was. I didn't need to "go" anywhere. I was happy. I'd found my purpose, my God calling and I knew I could continue on this path indefinitely with great joy and bliss. I ask out of curiosity, "If I were to choose to leave the planet—which I am not choosing to do—where would I go?"

Back to the Pleiades, most specifically to enrapture self with the vibration of pure God tone. It is the Golden tone known with my name, the Golden Tone of Melchizedek. It is this

Golden Tone that the Pleiadian Emissaries of Light are holding for everyone on Earth. In the moment of perfect merging with Father Energy everyone will receive this gift once again.

Pleiades, I muse. Not much different than Mother Earth now that she is moving into her fifth dimensional ascension. The Pleiades I know holds the fifth to ninth dimensional vibration. Sounds like I'd be making a lateral move. No, when it's time for me to leave Mother Earth I hope to make the rise of consciousness to a much higher level, closer to the One. Lord Melchizedek continues:

But dear one, the rapture does not need to be given to you in your Pleiadian home. It can be descended onto you right here. That is why we say it is a choice point.

Yes! That is what I have been feeling—the rapture. I am experiencing the rapture you have brought to me. I choose not to depart. "Can this opportunity be done away with so there's no…" my voice trails off with no words to complete the sentence. I state my intention to Lord Melchizedek the Father of our Universe: "I choose life on Earth. I surrender that opportunity right now. You, my Father have offered me some fabulous work to do here on Earth. I ask that it be written in the Akashic records of my choice to continue service on Earth."

Yes, you have made the decision. It is now written in the Akashic records that you are staying on the planet to live the full expression of rapture in Earth's womb.

The Ascended Masters and Galactic Light Beings have invested extensive time and energy to re-form my body from carbon to crystalline. They have learned from me in this experimental process of descension, but there is so much more I can give. They have helped me clear my karmic entanglements, transmute (through the use of the Violet Flame) all the misqualified energy I created, and prepared me for service in this incredible time of Earth's ascension. It seemed awfully selfish to now say, "Thanks, but no thanks, I want to go home." I had asked for the opportunity NOT to present itself but that was not to be.

It is the endeavor of the Ascended Masters to pour as much of themselves, their nature, their qualities, their gifts and activities into the world of form. Lord Sananda has patiently taught me the way of Love. Last year, prior to August 8, 2008, a call went out via many networks. I received messages from the many Light Workers announcing this pivotal date. Lord Sananda had put out the call he was preparing to descend into the earthly realm by anchoring the light vibration Ray of Sananda. For millions of years from his master realm he had been preparing Earth for a series of initiations that would begin on this solar cycle 8:8:8. He would initiate the Feminine Christ body in the Gaia matrix, a process of awakening that began 2000 years ago. This would be the time the Divine Feminine and the Divine Masculine would merge as One for the full embodiment of Earth as the Christ Being.

This would begin a new time cycle. Sananda has guided and protected mankind and our precious Mother Gaia and carefully assisted us through each challenge of duality. The date chosen was 8:8:8. Each of us received this state of actualization and consciousness on that day. Everyone was initiated and their DNA and Light bodies were time-coded according to when the Ray will be personally actualized. For some, the Ray of Sananda will be activated in future lifetimes. Those who were ready to actualize this new consciousness have begun to speak the messages awakened in them, the messages that will restore the spiritual connection and the messages that will guide the spiritual work to the new Golden Era. How coincidental to the opening of Stargates seeded 10,000 years ago, identified in 1877, and opened and activated in 2009.

I am sure Lord Sananda had his eye on me for many lifetimes. I'm a bit slow in my evolutionary process and surely had a few lifetimes of setbacks. In this lifetime however, I was truly ready to serve. It would be most disrespectful and ungrateful of me now to take these gifts and move off planet. Lord Sananda formally offered me the opportunity to be his Emissary of Light on August 8, 2008. I consciously chose "Yes" and he accommodated, allowing my contribution, my part in helping others to connect to the One Source. When an Ascended Master goes before the Karmic Board to petition utilizing one of his chelas to fulfill his plan, he approaches with full accountability for the relationship. An Ascended Master can only work through an unascended being—in this case, me. If the Karmic Board approves his plan and the chela does not deliver, the Ascended Master must personally make up for this energy exchange deficit. This can throw an Ascended Master back into the lower dimensions to rectify the deficit. The Law is the Law. The Karmic Board will not grant his wish unless he has an unascended being whose energies he can use. Ascended Masters' energies are best utilized in the higher cosmic realms; the Karmic Board knows this, but the Masters' Love for humankind is so great they ask to serve in the lower dimensions. In their mercy the Karmic Board approves. Ascended Masters make a commitment to the Karmic Board, assuring to make up for any energy the chela does not bring forth as promised. Free will is always the wild card when working with humanity. Should I choose to depart I would be going back on my commitment to Lord Sananda, something I would never do. My love for him is beyond description. And besides, I was just starting to have fun on this Earth plane.

Lord Melchizedek shared with me that creativity directed by Lord Sananda and others will come through me and for their benefit my work is best served on the planet. Certainly they could find another chela, but I have proven myself and they enjoy my company. Their preference is to work through me on Earth, but they would never interfere with my right to choose. I am told that as we begin our spiritual work in earnest we create triads with other beings. By working in triads the amplification is exponentially greater. I had a brief, very brief triad with Joshua David Stone and Alton Kadamon, both having ascended Earth and are now residing on the inner planes continuing their service there for our ascension. When I was first told I was working with them I thought it would be a long term, perhaps eternal relationship. It turned out to be quite short, occurring over a time just prior to this pilgrimage. We came together for a synergistic opening to shift my assemblage point, a vibration I now hold integrating me into higher echelons of Light. This triad is complete and I expect new triads of Masters affiliated with the Office of the Christ will come and go helping me in my call to service. We do, however, always retain the Master who personally accepted us as their chela for our ascension. I remain with Lord Sananda.

After leaving Chico we became stuck in a "four-wheel caravan" as Jim called the traffic we encountered. A single yellow line on this two-lane highway indicated passing was okay so we weren't breaking the law, just testing fate. We were behind a truck. There were cars coming in the opposite direction. We could see them, but we had enough time to pass. Jim pulled out. He had not been able to see the car in front of the truck he was passing. Too late! He was committed. Now he must pass two cars in the time he allotted for one. We weren't driving our own car. It didn't have the engine power or pick up Jim was used to. He floored it, but without any increase in speed. Now we were dependent on the cars coming the other way to slow down in order to avoid colliding. Montanans are known for their fierce pride. They would rather be dead right than wrong. They were in the right. By rights they did not have to slow down. We were in the wrong. We shouldn't have been passing. One, one thousand, two, one…and we pulled in, back into our lane of safety, horns blaring, fingers wagging. Eye to eye we passed. Swear words I didn't know I remembered flew from my mouth. How quickly I drop into third dimensional language. It happened a second time, exactly the same—the choice point. And God, true to His word, honored mine.

It was getting late, 10:00 P.M. and the sun was sinking into the endless Montana sky. We had been up since dawn, having awakened 400 miles south of where we were now. We had opened *Spires Eyes*, traveled back through the pack of tourists in Yellowstone Park, enjoyed a hearty lunch, reminisced about our honeymoon days 30 years earlier, soaked our sore cramped muscles in the Chico Hot Springs, and faced death on a lonely stretch of two lane road. We continued in quiet contemplation toward the final Stargate. I was inspired to call Judith. Luckily we were in one of the few places with cell coverage in this sea of wheat fields and I was able to receive the final piece of divinely guided information to Stargate #7.

Judith, in San Diego, answered on the first ring. Our cell connection was bad. "Give me ten minutes," she said, knowing this was important. We each knew our communication was being directed by Source greater than both of us; she selflessly dropped what she was doing, enjoying dinner with a friend, and drove to the beach. Judith is a true messenger of God. She is selfless, sometimes to the point of physical exhaustion, yet when she knows she is called by God nothing stops her. So off to the beach she headed to ground herself in the waves and sand and bring forth the following message for me to continue:

> *There's something happening with the DNA. I am feeling a lot happening in my body right now. I'm seeing that when you open the Stargate there is going to be a DNA descended through the Stargate to the heart of Mother Gaia—a 13 strand golden DNA helix. It is a new cosmic DNA. When you open the seventh Stargate you are to set the intention to anchor this golden helix. It is the DNA of the Cosmic Christ.*

Yes, this all makes sense. I know this is the Stargate of pure Christ Light. It is the Cosmic Christ Light, Christ Ray we are opening. I know it is Lord Sananda, the Cosmic Christ who is the Ascended Master of this Stargate. Yes, this is in perfect attunement with the information I was given before we began this journey. It is the final integration point on our pilgrimage, the pinnacle, the crown chakra of Illumination. This Stargate holds the integrity of the Christ Consciousness for the entirety of the streams of Love and Light. This is the activation point of Mother Earth's DNA. This is the moment Gaia, a living entity like all of us, will receive the cosmic codes for her ascension.

Whoa! I am dropped to my knees by our part in the play of this cosmic drama. What an immense privilege. Once the DNA has been seeded to the 13th strand in Mother Earth, all of humankind will have access to this higher DNA to assist them on their ascension path. This is huge with enormous consequence for the acceleration of our ascension process. No gift is given without a gift being received. Gift Given, Gift Received. These words have followed me on my spiritual path and until now I was never completely cognizant of their true meaning. *Whoa!*

Let me share with you how Master Lord Kuthumi explained the concept of DNA to me. When we return to our point of origination, back to pure Source God energy from whence we first sparked, our DNA level will be 24-strand. This is our pure God Essence. When we hold 24-strand DNA all of our gifts and abilities are restored and fully accessible. When we hold 24-strand DNA we are fully able to ascend and move totally out of the frequency of Earth, to be in etheric form. This is the stream of consciousness which is allowed when we move back into the perfect image and similitude of God—the Adam Kadmon body. The perfected Light Body is a perfect 24 strand DNA. Think of DNA as a capacity element. It is bringing in the streams which hold Light. When the fall of mankind occurred, its original 24 strand DNA devolved into the consciousness of a 2 strand DNA. Our full capacity for intelligence, for genius, the capacity for Peace or whatever Divine God attribute we wished to access, all of our abilities devolved from this 24 strand DNA to a very limited 2 strand DNA. We have truly been living in the dark, shrouded and veiled from our God Presence, our Divinity, and all the gifts that are our birthright as Sons of God. What a blessing to be living in this time of awakening to our I AM Presence!

As Joshua David Stone shared his ascension process with his readers, I am sharing mine with you in the hope it will be as valuable and helpful on your personal journey. I am presently ascending toward a 21-strand DNA—a journey over eons of time and hundreds of incarnations. I am humbled to know my God Self, to stand fully empowered in my I AM Presence, to be so close to home. I know I have another initiation and it is looming. It will be the resurrecting of every aspect of my heart chamber that has ever been closed to Eternal Love in this dimension through all time. It will be a celebration of the release of the last of the wounds of my heart. This will be most difficult. This experience is what is meant in the Bible when the stories are told of Christ speaking about piercing the heart. When the heart is pierced any and all forms of wounding are revealed as anti-God substance and are released. It will be an initiation through darkness. Frankly, I would prefer the type of initiation where I am given a beautiful white robe, crown and scepter, but I am prepared for this final unification. I am grateful to my Masters for the preview.

Bringing the heart into total self love can only be accomplished through feelings in the emotional body. It can never be completed through the intellectual aspect of the mind. I wish! An emotional trigger will be required. Translation: anger, abandonment, irritation, resentment, self-reproach, unworthiness and loss—all those ungodly emotions I prefer to think I have transcended. My next step to full transfiguration will most likely occur shortly after my completion of the pilgrimage. I now hold enough Light from this journey to face this next initiation. I will be watched, guided and protected from being swept away into any form of oblivion or static space we might call purgatory, limbo or the bardo. The thought of having to incarnate many more times to rectify this last step keeps me on course and gives me the courage to face the parts of me I shut off for whatever misguided reasons. It is about reclaiming that which I have abandoned, something I know I have done many times over many lifetimes. Now I will have the opportunity to bring back into the womb of my Mother Self those soul fragments I abandoned. Where I have failed before, I now have opportunity for unification. My ego punishes me for my past mistakes, tries to pull me into self loathing, but I do not listen. I have long ago forgiven myself for the times I freely chose to learn my lessons through shadow rather than Light.

This will, hopefully, be the last time I will learn through struggle. That is no longer my way. In the past, many of us chose to learn through the vortex of the descended Christ energy, the shadow and duality which were in opposition or in juxtaposition and without symmetry to the Father. This form of learning is no longer necessary. I have done the work to release my childhood anxiety and the wounded state of the child. She is ready to play. I recognize it will be a challenge and I am preparing myself with prayer and assistance from Lord Sananda not to trip on this final step into Oneness. The final unification of my soul is to be faced with ultimate self Love and forgiveness and I thank the generous human being who volunteered to be the catalyst, the trigger for my heart opening. In the end, it will be celebration of the purity of the heart coming into the white flame.

While absolving my abandonment issues I stumbled upon an "Aha!" moment with respect to the word abandon. A-band-on. A band one. A band of one. The true meaning of abandon is "a band of one." A band being a family or soul group. Abandon is simply moving from one soul group to another, neither better or worse than the other. Abandon was simply a misconceived form of atonement. Abandonment issues, the unforgiven child, the disowned mother are all the stories and untruths we created to separate from our Self and fragment our souls. They are nothing more than our made up illusions. They do not exist in God's Reality. But since at some time on my time on Earth during some incarnation I chose to make up this false reality, I must rectify and release this misconception to come Home. Home, another wonderful acronym—**H**eaven **O**n **M**other **E**arth!

Where were we? Oh yes, back to the message from Judith. It's still Thursday night. Jim found a grocery store and went shopping for late night supplies. I sit in the parking lot and continue with Judith:

> *When the Stargate opens I see a 13 strand golden DNA helix descending into the Stargate to encode the Earth Mother with the 13 strand DNA. It is changing the hologram of the DNA structure system of Earth. Not only is this the surrender point of Chief Joseph and his people but in ancient times it was a birthing place.*
>
> *There is a womb there. Look for the crescent shaped womb in the Earth. It's here Mother Earth will receive her new DNA encodements through this seventh Stargate. Yes, how synchronistic. The Stargate is located at an ancient birthing site and we are birthing the 13 strand golden DNA in Mother Earth.*

That's the message. It's late. Judith is tired. I'm exhilarated. When I communicate to Source energy, I am in my pure God essence. It's a party I never want to end.

Jim has been a tireless scout. This is not his passion as it is mine. He enjoys Padres games, NBA playoffs, NASCAR and spending time with me. Well, he's had plenty of time with me lately, and his protection, guiding and caring on this journey have been a selfless act of Love. There were very few times on our pilgrimage when fatigue would rule, but this was one of those times. He's tired. Jim is impeccable in all he does. He is always safe. To have experienced such a close call with death hundreds of miles back took its toll on his Peace—although he will never admit it.

As I acknowledged, I have spent years and years and thousands and thousands of dollars hiring countless spiritual guides to attain my current level of "self love" mastery. My ego still holds plenty of influence, so I am not quick to relinquish this Love of self by acknowledging that when tired or hungry I can be just a "bit" difficult. At the choice point I had erupted in fear. Jim in his patient way, allows, allows, allows and so we dance the dance we have created over 33 years—he allowing, me expressing. Together we make our way to a place of Peace. Jim's fond of jokingly quoting Toby Keith: "Only Me and God Love Her!"

Past the point of fatigue, we arrived in Havre sixteen hours after traveling from Jenny Lake. It was 10:30 P.M., well beyond our dawn to dusk routine. There were so many bugs on the windshield we could barely see. We can drive in San Diego for months and never hit a single bug. Jim was tired and the bugs were a non-amusing distraction. I hadn't driven a mile on the entire pilgrimage. Jim was happy in the driver's seat, tired or not, but for the first time he was showing signs of exertion. The energizer bunny was ready for a recharge. Unfortunately, it wouldn't be tonight. He had hit the wall. We were looking forward to a good night's rest. We'd called ahead using the *AAA TourBook,* locating three star lodging, the best in Havre, so we booked the last room. "How could a town like Havre be sold out?" we queried. It's in the middle of wheat country where people are few. No one around for miles and miles. Only a state high school tournament could sell out Havre. We were relieved and happy we had the foresight to call ahead. Silly us!

After checking in we opened the door to our room and were accosted by a stench rivaling a boys' locker room. By the scent we could tell it had been a party room and the revelers in their exuberance made off with the mini-fridge filled with the remaining beer they hadn't been able to consume the night before. We could imagine the scenario that had unfolded just from the reek of the room. Now the front desk clerk's apology for the missing mini-fridge made sense. The gaping hole gave clues to the previous wild night. Oh, the season of high school graduation. Had we not been so tired we would have rejoiced in their fun—an all-nighter celebrating emancipation—but in our mood it was just another irritation. Thank God for our own down comforter and pillows. We turned on the air conditioner trying to clear out the stagnation. Opened the window. For the first time there was not much to say to each other. A sideways glance from Jim and I knew it would be best to crawl quickly under the sheets and sleep it off, each coping with our fatigue in our own way. Each thinking "Let's just get through this night without saying something we'll regret." Get our heads on the pillows as fast as we can. Luckily we were toward the end of the trip. Had we experienced these feelings earlier on it would have been a longer long journey. We can laugh about it now, but at the time we had clearly dropped into third dimension. Finally, lights out.

Only to find our room overlooked the railroad tracks. Not just the railroad tracks with an occasional freight train passing through—THE Burlington Northern Railroad Locomotive Repair Facility. The only place in the country where they bring all the broken down locomotives and put them in a warehouse (a huge building that could easily house a 747). A place where the mechanics work ALL NIGHT. Once they get them running they let them run and run and run. Ah the hum of a railroad locomotive through the windows and walls of a room just a stone's throw away. We shut the window, not blocking the sound one decibel. The heat became oppressive. We woke up in a sweat, opened the window and placed pillows over heads. Hey God, who's the travel agent on this leg?

Friday, May 29, 2009

By the Grace of God we have come to notice that every morning, regardless of the length or difficulty of the previous day, we are refreshed and energized. Today is no different except not only are we refreshed, we are exuberant. We are in celebration mode. We are coming to the completion. "Today will be ecstasy because we'll be at the end of our pilgrimage," says Jim. "We will leave behind all of the seeds of our labor and they will ripen to fruit for those who will come in future millenniums. We ask those who come to eat the fruit so lovingly planted to share what they receive with everyone and everything throughout the Universe." A serious epitaph which he ends in his usual humorous fashion. "And now we Tolo Portal." His way of saying, "Let's move on!"

We pack up, say good riddance to the room we will never see again and jump in the car. Jim is prompted to look at the odometer. I had written down the beginning mileage when we departed Spokane, our official "start" of the Stargate pilgrimage. The odometer read 9,569 miles. Ending mileage at Havre—11,446 miles. Total mileage—1877 miles. The year of Chief Joseph's Exodus—1877. Coincidence? Not even! We smile at each other, a new smile we have come to know, new to our repertoire of expressions. We are God knowing. No doubting Thomas these two.

The sun is shining brilliantly. In the wheat fields of Montana the sky is endless. They call Montana "Big Sky Country" for a reason. Growing up I took this distinction for granted, but after years in the smog and fog of Southern California I've grown to cherish the expansive brilliant blue of my home state. We can see forever. We can't see the wind but it's blowing. There is nothing to stop its momentum except the occasional grain silo. It's beautiful from the inside of the car. The rolling plains are elegant in their simplicity. It's early; even the ranchers are still at home breakfasting after sunrise chores. We cherish the feeling of owning the world.

We head to Chinook then south another sixteen miles to the site of Bear's Paw, the last point on Chief Joseph's exodus—his point of surrender—just forty miles short of the Canadian border and freedom. Joseph felt he had a few days advance of his pursuers and this would be a good time to build camp. Snow was beginning to fall, food was scarce and his people were worn. Here, unaware that all was being orchestrated according to the Divine plan, the Nez Perce were besieged by the Army. With losses mounting, on October 5, 1877, four months since the first skirmishes at White Bird, Joseph surrendered his rifle to General Howard ending the wrongful expulsion from their home over 1,100 miles away.

Not all of the tribes were in consensus; surrender or continue flight? Here signifies the divergence of two paths, two spiritual journeys; one of Peace, Chief Joseph *"I will fight no more forever"* and Chief White Bird's flight to Freedom. Divine Will would allow neither. The time of Peace and Freedom was not to be for Chief Joseph or Chief White Bird. In the end, Chief Joseph surrendered at Bear's Paw along with approximately two-thirds of his people. Chief White Bird and 150 of his tribe fled camp and succeeded in reaching Canada to the home of the Sioux. However, Chief White Bird's escape was not his assumption to Freedom. For the two great Chiefs and the Nimiipuu, the People of Peace—the time of Peace and Freedom was not to be.

In the future this point of surrender, this Stargate *Ascended Earth* will be a portal where many will choose their ascension. It is the last integration, the pinnacle point holding the integrity of the entirety of the total beam. It is the crown chakra, the illumination of the lotus. This is the place where we will encode the 13 strand golden DNA into the land in order that it can be brought into the heart of Mother Gaia for her ascension and ours.

In last night's message from Judith I was guided to look for a womb formation in the landscape. We found it easily, obvious to even the most novice readers of landscape formations. Facing us was a crescent shaped bluff providing a protective barrier for the meadow below. We were in the area; now to determine the exact location. We stop the car and before we even get out a haze of mosquitoes surround the vehicle. Even the prairie winds do not deter these tough little guys. So we scout from the front seat.

To the left we notice two trees. From this distance, about a half-mile off, we can't tell if they are large overgrown bushes or stunted trees. Of course nothing is trimmed or groomed; in their natural state some bushes and trees are indiscernible except to the arborist's trained eye. Whatever they are, trees or bushes, they are calling us. While it appears lovely from the inside of the car, when we step out we are bombarded with icy wind and swarms of mosquitoes. Jim immediately remembers the clary sage essential oil. It works like a charm on the mosquitoes. What a Scout!

We remind ourselves that once we get to the Stargate both the wind and mosquitoes will disappear. The trees are within sight, but like a desert oasis appearance is deceiving. The eye can see forever into the vastness so what appears close by could be miles and miles. We bundle up to protect from the biting wind, but more so to spare any exposed flesh from the hungry critters, and head out. The brilliant sunshine is misleading. The temperature hovers in the low 50s. Wind chill drops it to the 30s.

As we follow the path toward the trees we see a hawk circling the area. As we watch a second hawk joins his flight pattern. Our guides are pointing the way. When a hawk shows up he is telling us to stay alert and focused. Ignore the details and take a look from above to gain a greater perspective. Pay close attention to your surroundings. We are about to receive an important latent message from the hawk to Chief Joseph: *Stop trying to change the situation and accept things as they are. It is time for Peace; time to surrender.* The hawk also warns us to be mindful of dark forces at play. This is a battle site and a gravesite and the correlating energies are here. I had been assured the energy would be clear and pure for our final work today. This is NOT White Bird, Idaho, the place of Souls Knolls.

We cross a small creek and stop to bless the waters with Peace Waters, asking the creek to flow blessings to all this land. With this simple acknowledgement to the elementals the wind begins to subside. For eons the elementals have tirelessly and selflessly kept our bodies and that of Mother Earth alive, without our knowing or even an occasional expression of appreciation. It is time to recognize their selfless service.

There are three types of Intelligent Life evolving on Planet Earth—Angels, Human Beings and Elementals. Each contributes to the Love and well-being of the other and together they weave the spiritual bridge from the Heart of Mother Gaia to the Heart of God. The elementals are under the direction of the devas and their purpose is to serve mankind. In return they are promised their own evolution. The elementals are selfless servants. Unlike mankind they do not have free will but are charged with obeying the every direction of man, materializing out of Earth, Air, Water, and Fire the nourishment required to repair, replenish and keep our bodies alive, as well as making our life happy and harmonious. They also direct Mother Earth's weather patterns. There is much to share about the elementals, this kingdom we rely on unknowingly. They are rarely spoken of and little acknowledged for their importance to us.

I sing to the mosquitoes asking them to spare us, but it's not necessary. The magic of the clary sage has already begun to work. A beautiful red winged blackbird greets us with a song. There's a chorus of birds and a single hawk is still circling the trees. Open plains; we can see "as far as the eye can see." It is beautiful, but deceiving, probably one of the harshest Stargate areas we've encountered. We arrive at the trees, the Stargate Keeper. Nestled below, buried in prairie grass we find a rock. This is the Grandmother's Rock, the Mother Stone foretold of before we arrived. I have no question this is it. I can feel it. It is here. This is the place mentioned in the message I received from Chief Joseph many weeks ago:

I am happy to be with you. It is a good reunion. It is a good time to come home. I AM Joseph, Chief of the Nez Perce people from the beginning of time and the beginning of this nation. You will come to the place where before we surrendered you left your sacred bundle. You will know the place. It will be close to the proximity where I surrendered. There you will touch the sacred Grandmother Stone and your medicine ways will return through you to the people. For you know you are a Gateway of Light.

This Stargate will create a meeting point of the souls. Those who were wounded in the past can heal and that which was gifted in the future of Peace, this proud lineage, will again be as Peace Keepers, not as warriors, as we were before we were forced to defend our land. Aho. I have spoken.

So here it is; the place where I was told I had left my sacred medicine bundle on that fateful day. And here is where I will retrieve and reclaim all my God-given gifts, the ones I surrendered, not just in this lifetime, but through all my embodiments when the veils of forgetfulness concealed my knowing. Today the veils will be lifted and I will know my true God Self once again. Today I am Re-membering, uniting soul fragments into One with my I AM Presence. The return of the Prodigal Son—this remembrance brings me to my knees, tears to my eyes.

This is not the first lifetime I have surrendered my healing powers to the false illusion of my ego. During many lifetimes, afraid I would use them for reasons other than the expansion of

God's Light, I gave them up. Ignored them; buried them. I was afraid of my power—if unharnessed it could not be controlled. A part of me could not accept my Goodness, the pure Light of God that I AM. Lifetime after lifetime I lived as a non-adept, repeating the vow to never use my God-given abilities for fear of misuse. I did not trust myself with such power. At one time I had created the illusion of wielding this power in a destructive, harmful manner. Better to not have it than to use it improperly, so I shut down. Today I am turning the power back on!

Relinquishing my power was not a new issue with me. I was quick to give it away for fleeting approval. I had been working on this consciously for years with guides and teachers, ironically giving my power to them and paying them to take it! Through channeling sessions, past life regressions and journaling, I sought the key that would open the lock, giving myself permission to reclaim my powers, the ones I had suppressed for reasons I did not know. It wasn't important to know the details of each lifetime of misuse or why. All I know is that I relinquished them lifetime after lifetime. Now I am being gifted the reclamation. The only one way to reclaim my power is to go to my inner knowing of my God Self. I am ready. I have relinquished my false ego humility and I stand fully in my Goddess Light. Each step of this journey prepared me for this moment of acceptance of my crown and scepter. I will reclaim my bundle and leave behind this new sacred bundle for mankind, so others too, in the name of Love can reclaim their God Reality.

We lift the big rock and underneath is a small stone the shape of a pyramid. It is my sign; it is where I left my bundle. Next to the stone there is grass everywhere except for a small area where nothing is growing. Jim says, "This is the spot." And so we begin. The wind and mosquitoes have disappeared. The hawk and the companion hawks guide are also gone. For the last time at the site of this Mother Stone we open our sacred bundle of supplies to begin. Aware of the battleground surroundings, I pay special attention to my amethyst crystal asking St. Germain to transmute all misqualified energy. This is a special Stargate, our last, so I break out the essential oil, Sandalwood. It's my favorite—preciously expensive! I use it to bring in the highest sacred vibration and mostly because I love it. We bless ourselves with the holy water from Lourdes and Peace Waters to bring us into the Immaculate Concept and receiving place of all the blessings of the Divine Mother. We energetically tune in to this fertile place of birthing and to our job of bringing in the 13 strand golden DNA helix for the encoding of Mother Earth as she ascends to her highest level.

The wind picks up but we are unaffected by it. We sprinkle the sacred leaf and ask for this land to continually provide plenty for all who live here and the passersby. We sprinkle the sacred earth from Chimayo and give thanks to Judith for bringing us to this point and awakening us to this beautiful calling asked of us by God. Finally, we share the blue cornmeal so the wheat harvest will be plentiful and the farmers and ranchers will enjoy unlimited abundance, for our sustenance and for all they desire from the fruits of their labor. For the final time, we take a piece of sacred ash given to me by my friend, Dave, and rub it on the palm of our left hand. This is a ritual we adopted along the way to open to the wisdom of the coalition of all the Indian elders and leaders. We pour the Lady of Lourdes holy water into the impression of the rock and cover the bundle with the Mother Stone. We open the Stargate, the crown chakra, the Christ Ray. Feelings of jubilance, ecstasy, celebration and exultation wash over us. We sing, realizing an incredible Lightness. The words of our songs flow. It is the miraculous feeling of giving birth.

Following the path on our return we discover markers where many of the Nez Perce warriors had fallen and the sites where their family's tepee stood. Funny how we had not noticed these markers on our walk to the Stargate—this is as it should be. There are two purposes for this visit: one to birth and anchor new DNA for a new beginning, and the other to honor those who paved the way to Peace. Each site is indiscreetly marked by a stainless steel post, a surveyor's stake. We stop at each one and with a prayer and the sign of Peace we place the stone, Danburite. Danburite is a shiny, colorless stone which assists with angelic communication and increases the ability for interdimensional travel. Interestingly, it is of the element Wind. Its gift is to uplift one to higher spiritual vibrations. For those souls who may still be holding on to this time and space, Danburite is a beautiful gift and tool for release. Now these souls can go from their temporary resting places to the highest Source of Creation allowing them to take flight instantly. It feels like most of them have moved on. I had asked God to prepare the field before we arrived so we would not endure what we did at Souls Knolls. I was assured this land had been healed and was awaiting the celebration of our arrival. This Stargate opening would be a time of celebration. Gift Given, Gift Received.

When we reached the site of Chief Joseph's tepee we were humbled by his presence; his selfless service to his people, and the Peace he so fervently sought in his lifetime. We left an offering and moved on in reverence. We placed Danburite at the gravesite of Chief Looking Glass, at the gravesite of Peu Peu Wah Nap Tah, the teepee of Never Go Hunting, at the tepee of San Pu Ma and the tepee of Tu Nah Ho. We are reminded of the last episode of the television show *Survivor* when each of the final remaining contestants walk the torch trail of those eliminated. "Nothing's sacred!" we laugh. Even though this is serious work everything has a feeling of lightness and fun, a good reminder that when we are doing sacred ceremony in the name of God it should never be somber. God is Light and Love. If we are not in laughter, we are not in Love. Even though this is a memorial site the atmosphere is jovial. The land has been healed and it is a time of celebration as we open this Stargate, *Ascended Earth.*

Back at the trees, Jim noticed others had left ribbons, prayer flags and scarves tied to their branches. Tattered and torn by the wind, they were joyful in their breezy way. Jim suggested we return to the site and tie a second sacred bundle to the branch of the tree containing the three Pleiadian stones, the rose quartz, the clear quartz, illuminite, the dove feather and Ascension Keys. What a beautiful idea! We headed back down the trail and tied the bundle with 13 knots. The first seven knots to represent the seven Stargates we had opened—*Dolphin's Halo, Ancient Wisdom, Swallows Window, Heart of the Golden Rose, Peace Waters, Spires Eyes* and *Ascended Earth.* The 13 knots represented the 13 strand golden DNA. The bundle represented the remembrance that there is life after life and our journey never ends.

As hard as it is to accept what ought not be—the inequities and suffering of the Nez Perce—all was in Divine timing. On his spiritual path to fulfill his destiny Chief Joseph's final destination was Lake Louise in Canada, to anchor the eighth and final Stargate, the *Ascension Gate.* Had he reached his destination Peace would have prevailed throughout the world. The time was simply not right.

The Nez Perce as a people in 1877 could not go to this sacred place because they were still living in a consciousness of survival. This final Stargate can only be reached through Grace. Theirs was a way of protection, the way of survival. Their choices were made from feelings of fear causing the rivers to dry up and the food to become scarce. Only until survival is no longer the focus of the human mind and the way of Peace is at hand can someone lead the people to the eighth Stargate, to the eighth sacred place of Ascension. That time is now.

Oh the richness, the beauty, the sweetness of the rivers filled with salmon once again. The berries ripe and plump upon the bushes in the fall harvest. And the bear grease given and not taken by Grandmother Bear.

This is a sacred place of geographical memory in our hearts. We are taught to "turn ourselves around" in reverence and prayer upon entry into sacred space. This prayerful act keeps us ever mindful of the presence of our Creator as we reach out to the heart . . . to know that we are always truly "one".

Monday, June 1, 2009

Having taken a few days to rest and rejuvenate, we are back where it all began at the heart of Whitefish Lake giving thanks for a transformational, transcendent experience. I had called Judith. It was she who opened this opportunity and like a good soul journeyer I reported back. She had a message for me from Chief Joseph:

My daughter, my granddaughter it is I Joseph that speaks to you now. Throughout the ages there was a division between the Star Nations. The hoop was broken and the migration routes ceased. That division was a mirror of the Heavens and mirrored the wars on Earth in many places in many ways. The Star Chiefs from these many star nations formed a Council of Light in ancient times. The Chiefs awaited the call when the voices of the Thunder Beings carried the message to the Star Councils. Hearing this message they journeyed through the star systems to join with their earthly spirits. At the activation of each Stargate an Ancient Star Chief was awakened and journeyed with you on your pilgrimage pathway. These Chiefs awakened other creation energies; energies that are mirrored from the Stars to Earth and from the Earth to the Heavens.

They have emerged from these seven sacred Stargates. At Bear's Paw, which you call Stargate Ascended Earth, these seven Ancient Masters rejoined me to form an Alliance of Peace in the Cosmic order and on the Earthly plane. What transpired in the spirit realm is mirrored at the 7th Stargate.

The People of Peace are given to the rivers, the streams, the trees, the Earth and the gardens, given for new songs. You now will return to San Diego and at this anchor point the Pleiadian Stargate will be activated. The Ancient Star Chiefs will reunite and you will open the Infinity Gateway. June 13, 2009 is the day. This is the Infinity Gateway.

There are rivers of life that will flow on the Earth that were dried up, rivers of life that will flow from the Infinity Gate seeding the body of Mother Earth with sacred life force. From the Mothers of the Ancients and the Cosmic Councils, the Mothers' milk will flow through the rivers of life feeding the spirits that wait for this gift to awaken.

Granddaughter, daughter, sister, friend you have come full cycle. And this all has come to be in the passing of time which is infinite and immortal. The Infinity Gate lives for all time in the heart of Turtle Island, in the heart of Mother Earth, in the heart of the Divine Mother's Light, the heart of Creation.

This gift is given. Amma Moskue is the name to this Gateway of Light, this Infinity Gate—Amma Moskue—I ask you to take this name for yourself now as a sacred name that I give you. I ask you to accept this name and to hold it sacred. Share this name with others when you feel you can share your soul and the Light of your soul in a moment of joy when you know that the name Amma Moskue will be received with Love. I am Joseph. I am your brother. Aho.

This is the fulfillment of the Native American Prophecy of the Eagle and the Condor that tells how we will come together and reunite as one. These places are the heart of the spiritual alliance brought to Earth 10,000 years ago, uniting all of mankind who were separated by their own differences.

With this new information we are ready to open and activate the last two anchor points. Our pilgrimage is not yet over. It will culminate at its origination point in San Diego completing the circle of infinity. But first we must open the pathway for the pure of heart, the *Gateway OM* in Whitefish. We head north on Highway 93 to mile marker 151, turning left toward Upper Stillwater Lake and the Finger Lake trailhead. We follow the gravel road over the bridge above the railroad tracks. It's a bumpy road and requires a high clearance vehicle. As we pass over the Stillwater River and the railroad tracks the Forest Service sign guides us around a hairpin turn to the left opening to a turnout for parking. We park at the trailhead and begin our second-to-last adventure. We've enjoyed the enlightenment each Stargate has awakened in us; we feel the end coming near—a bittersweet feeling for us both.

We are preparing to open the Great Gateway, the Home Gate, The Peace Gate, the Love Gate, *Gateway OM*. We start down the trail. We know it well. It's one of our favorite hikes. It is wooded, moist and shaded by the overgrowth. "Bear country," I think to myself and quickly begin a prayer to all the animals we now know as friends to welcome and protect us. It is early morning and the air is chilled from the night. We're bundled up, not only from the early morning chill but from the mosquitoes hungry for blood. The sun is not quite bright enough to send them to their shelters so they own the trail for now. We're prepared for them and spray ourselves amply with the beautiful essential oils from Amrita. As the trail forks, we follow the signs to the right. I've been lost here a few times. Thankfully, so have others and a new sign has been posted signaling to the directionally challenged like me.

Usually this time of year the trail and meadows are filled with wildflowers. It has been an extremely harsh winter and the signs of spring are still hidden. Only a few flowers have ventured forth. The mosquitoes still rule and the bears are still coming from their winter hibernation. The bear bells give me comfort as I sing and chant our way to the lake. As we near Finger Lake the caw of the raven greets us. Jim caws back perfectly in tune, indiscernible from the real. I joke with Jim it's not the first time that his girlfriend is calling. Jim and the raven have long been mates, each singing their song to the other.

We circle to the right of the lake and come to a rock outcropping in the shape of a crescent. We've learned to be sensitive to crescent shaped formations; they mark an important place, a womb for Mother Earth. We've learned our lessons well and acknowledge this guidepost for our arrival to *Gateway OM.* Across from the crescent rock outcropping is a huge, ancient tree, struck by lightning, but still standing. Only its trunk remains, but it is magnificent in its splendor and we pay homage.

We are greeted by a bumble bee and instantly connect to sacred resonance. Throughout our pilgrimage the bees have appeared when we are perfectly attuned to the high frequencies of consciousness. They appear out of the blue signifying we are in sacred resonance, verifying harmony of Peace and Love. The bees connect us to the Universal OM, the Universal tone. They carry the sound frequency of God affirming to us that we are One, in tune and connected. Reliably they show up after we open each Stargate. We tone the full name Waneen Wan Yan: Completion, Full Circle, One. They tone with us and then move on. Hereafter, the bees will have special meaning to me, a small sign from God to acknowledge my true "Bee-ing."

We find the *Gateway OM* at the end of the trail, near water's edge; back to the Peace waterways of Montana. There's an outcropping directly above the Gateway looking much like a Chief. His forehead, eyes, nose and smile are clearly visible. It is very calm here. The first thing we notice is the change in temperature. Gratefully, we had been followed by the wind which helps to keep the mosquitoes at bay. Here, there is no wind. Interestingly, even without the wind there are no mosquitoes. The small lakeshore area is in full bloom with purple, yellow and white flowers. The only place trailside where spring is in bloom. No surprise. Seven Stargates back we discovered the Stargates hold unique energy. It can only be described as the Garden of Eden as we would imagine it. The bees are back to greet us. They dance from flower to flower savoring the nectar of each bloom.

The bees are the Greeters of this *Gateway OM* and no wonder. To be here, and for this anchor point to open, all must be in sacred resonance and pure of heart. Looking back to the lake, it is sided by two large rock walls resembling the birth canal, the point of origination. This is the point of perfection, where we leave all life's incarnations, miscreations and rejoin with pure Source/Mother/Father God. We leave behind all lifetimes, everything that has taken us away from our origination and our God Presence. From this point forward any who enter must be pure of heart and dedicated to the One pure Source of Light. It is the Great *Gateway OM.*

This is the first Gateway where we were not given any prior channeled information of the energy we would feel or its vibration. We're on our own to determine why and what it is we're here to open. It is obvious to us and apparent that the Stargate gifts awaiting Mother Gaia, mankind and us personally are the perfection, the wholeness and the purity of heart. We feel the point of origination, the freeing of all the misqualified use of energy in all time, space and dimension. We feel the sacred resonance. We feel the Supreme Love, the Supreme Peace. The lake is still. The wind is calm, the mosquitoes are gone. It is a place of perfect serenity. We call it the Great Gateway—the *Gateway OM.*

We bring out our sacred bundle for the last time until we return to San Diego. We consecrate ourselves and this land in final preparation. We're both wishing this journey and the gifts and feelings it has opened in us will continue forever. We thank the animals for making our passage safe. The insect world is very present. Bees, dragonflies and mosquitoes have been our greeters and helpers at this Gateway. Now we're greeted for the first time by a little black spider. Not surprising. A spider showing up means this is an opportunity to access our deepest wisdom and integrate it into our knowing. He asks us to be willing to explore other dimensions and realities. And we are! We sprinkle the last of the blue cornmeal into the lake and are delighted by the minnows who surface to feed. What joy—they love the cornmeal! We sprinkle the sacred soil of Chimayo, the home of

Judith around us and in the lake. We bless and give thanks to Judith for being the perfect channel so we could manifest God's desire on Earth. We connect our hearts to her heart. Since this is a place of sweet restoration and pure bliss we anoint ourselves with lavender and rosemary. We collect the waters from Finger Lake to bless other waterways as we journey on in the future.

Only the pure of heart can cross through this Gateway. Going back to the point of origination we rebirth into the Light from which we come. It is the beginning and the end, the alpha and omega, the return to Oneness, the circle complete. It is Peace and perfection. We have entered the sacred heart. There is no turning back. The doorway to darkness has been closed. Those who have not yet entered will continue their journeys and lessons and this gateway to God will open for them when their hearts become pure. This is the seeding of Forgiveness and Love. It is the descension of the Divine Perfection. When the gate of origin opened I was able to see all of my many lifetimes, incarnations, miscreations that were not of pure God Essence being let go, one by one. As if dressed in costume, in a play of make-believe experiences I disrobed, piece by piece, lifetime by lifetime until I was left standing bare, pure at my point of origination, my pure God Essence, One with Source. The veils had been lifted. I was pure heavenly Love experiencing the full embrace of God.

Ceremony ended we begin the scenic trek back to the car. On our return we are guided the entire way by blue luminescent dragonflies. The messages are indeed clear from our animal and plant friends. It continues to astound us. Referring to our animal book we read that when a dragonfly shows up it means to be on the lookout for any deceit, delusions or false truth. This is the Gateway where only the pure of heart can enter. One must be in total Truth and Oneness. More than a simple change, the dragonfly—sister to the butterfly energy—tells us we are going through a major transformation.

We started our journey over ten days ago settling a large Pleiadian love stone collected from Torrey Pines San Diego into Whitefish Lake bringing these two conception points into one. We carried another large Pleiadian stone with us along the journey to every Stargate opening: *Dolphin's Halo, Ancient Wisdom, Swallows Window, Heart of the Golden Rose, Peace Waters, Spires Eyes, Ascended Earth* and *Gateway OM.* Now upon returning to Whitefish Lake I toss this Pleiadian stone carrying the vibration of our pilgrimage and the gifts of all the Stargates into the lake and step back to complete the infinity circle.

Upon our return to San Diego Judith had this to share:

Bear's Paw was not only the place of surrender by Chief Joseph, but is also near an ancient burial ground, a portal of the Ancients from 10,000 years ago. It has physically disappeared by now, but it is still there and it is called The Place of the Souls. It is there that the Ancestors came and I see a procession of Ancestor Spirits joining you as you move along this pathway of exodus to the Stargate of Ascended Earth. At each Stargate that you opened previously a portal of the Star Nations was opened and from that point on a specific Star Chief journeyed with you. They have been your guardians along the way to help you.

Yes, we could feel their presence we just didn't know who they were.

And when you got to the seventh Stargate the last Star Chief joined the six who have been traveling with you. Seven Beings from this ancient place of the souls joined you. A call went out to the Ancients from each of these Stargates and they reunited again. This was a calling of the Star Nations together. They had not been united since ancient times. And so these seven Star Chiefs were with you and when they came together in Council there came a great Light upon the Earth and the DNA was able to encode that Light in the 13 golden strands. When that happened there was a call going out. It was an awakening of the Ancestor Spirits; the ones who wave in the wind. And I see that this was the place of the Eagle. Joseph was there in the center. And I see the seven ancient Star Beings standing around Joseph in the center. Above him is the Eagle and it forms a new medicine spirit wheel in this place. It is a living energy. The seven Star Chiefs and Joseph made a spirit wheel there.

One morning about a week later, I contacted my friend Bill. He has written the incredible story of his personal journey—*Biography of a Star Seed*—his story of what it is like to incarnate on Earth as a human being with the uncanny recollection of his life in Sirius before this embodiment. He has a gift of seeing Light frequencies and bringing these frequencies into consciousness. We collaborate together bringing in Light for each other, raising our consciousness and connecting to that pure Source energy which is so sublime.

Feeling the need to tangibly connect, I called Bill. What comes through me I am able to download to Bill; he brings Light frequencies into my consciousness and then I am able to download the higher frequency to him. Gift Given, Gift Received. This particular time Bill saw an entirely new Light vibration in my field, first as a group of beings and then as a galactic frequency. Yes, the Council of Eight—one Master Star Being from each Stargate and Chief Joseph—were with me now—always—opening me to greater awareness, greater heights of Being, greater Love. Yet again I drop my jaw and drop to my knees in gratitude.

Friday, May 29
Havre to Whitefish 253 miles

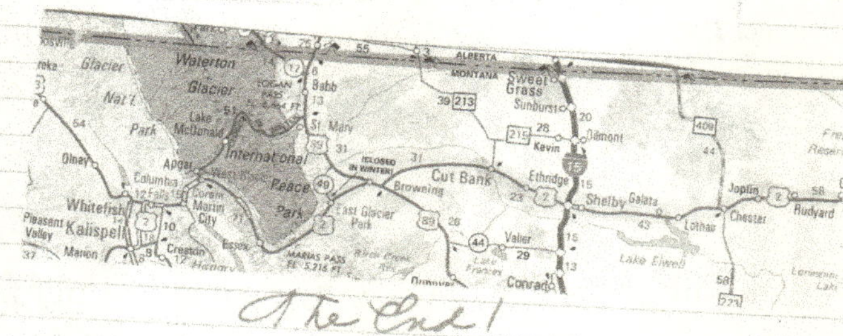

Saturday, June 13, 2009

On this day in San Diego at Torrey Pines Beach the sky is grey, the water is grey, there's no differentiation between sky and water. It's all infinite Oneness. We're here to open the second anchor point, *Infinity Gateway.* The master tone is Amma Moskue. Amma Moskue is the sacred name given to me by Chief Joseph—an enormous gift of gratitude given to me in my final message before opening this Stargate. It means Divine Mother of Completion. We sit next to the cliffs. Those who frequent this beach know the cliffs are faulty and very precarious. Anyone who visits is warned and knows not to sit or idle next to them. There have been rock falls and cliff collapses and deaths.

With this knowledge, I feel judgment as I sit here. I let that go. Just this once. The beach is crowded, even in this early hour on this grey morning. People are walking by but we are unobstructed. I call for the dolphins to see if they will join us in our ceremony. And we wait. We take yellow tipped ruby rose petals gathered from our home garden and one by one we release the petals; the waves take them into the ocean. As they merge with the surf we bless each Stargate one by one. The memories of our recent pilgrimage awaken in us, albeit bittersweet the journey has come to its conclusion. Next, we anoint ourselves with the holy waters of Lourdes and the Peace Waters of Whitefish and we pour the remainder into the ocean connecting the Peace Waters throughout the world.

I begin to play the crystal bowls and the tone vibrates through the sand. We are stopped by this amazing feeling. We can actually feel the vibration through our bodies. The Oneness has manifest. The crystal bowl is made of quartz crystal, the sand is quartz crystal and I, too, now carry the crystalline body structure, a process and gift of evolving from the carbon body to crystalline body in our ascension process. In harmony we sing our song.

We first came here, our favorite spot, a week ago to scope out a site and see if this was the anchoring place for the *Infinity Gateway* and the culmination of our pilgrimage. On that occasion we were greeted by five dolphins, three adults and two babies. The meeting point of the dolphins was in direct alignment with a crescent indentation of the cliff. We knew this was the spot. The dolphins circled as we watched from the shore and then they ceremoniously led the way down the beach keeping in time with us step-by-step back to our starting point. They followed us the entire half-mile keeping pace with our walk. It was magnificent to be in their presence, their honoring our slow movement, knowing they could be gone in seconds if they chose. We're calling for the dolphins, now, but it is not meant to be today.

As we begin our invocation two majestic black ravens circle overhead. Or are they peregrines who keep home on top of the bluff? Everything has become still, only in the distance are the birds singing our song. We were given the sacred tone "Amma Moskue" to open the *Infinity Gateway* anchor point. It is a new sacred resonance, one unfamiliar to us, so we go back to singing our love song Waneen Wan Yan for comfort's sake. The beach is crowded. Torrey Pines is a state park so we're cautious of being too flagrant with our ceremony and burying the sacred bundle. We're not allowed to walk on the cliffs. It's against the Forest Service regulations and the laws of common sense and safety.

Jim hastily scrambles up the cliff side, not far, but too far for knowing we shouldn't be doing this. But there is a perfect enclave which Jim knows is the spot. He places the sacred bundle in a little pocket in the rock cliffs. Our roles have changed—me Scout, Jim Sacred Journeyer. Gratefully the constant parade of people ceased for just those moments while we buried the bundle. We complete our prayer. Our job is done, but we keep lingering, holding on in these meaningful minutes. Our time in this unveiled reality has become so precious we choose not leave it just yet, not ready to re-enter into the third dimension world. So we sit, mesmerized by the ocean and the sound of the waves, never ending, never ceasing. Like the heartbeat, the rhythmic motion, the timekeeper of our Creator.

Saturday, June 28, 2009

From San Diego to Whitefish, the Stargate pilgrimage is fast becoming a memory. The encounters we thought we'd never forget are less vivid, fading. Perhaps this is as it should be. Living in the present moment has no past, no future. There is no memory in the Now. We returned to Finger Lake for a morning hike. It's one of our favorite spots, not too difficult but enough to know we've been hiking. The woods are thick; there's one meadow lush with moss and wildflowers. A month ago there were no meadow flowers. This time it was just finishing its bloom. In a few short weeks we had missed the explosion of colors, but we could imagine. We followed the trail to the head of Finger Lake a beautiful outcropping high above the lake where in the summer kids love to jump to show their prowess. Been there, done that. Three summers ago Jim had taken a 60 foot leap from a cliff into the Flathead River, curing him of that bravado real fast.

From the rock overhang we headed north circling the perimeter of the lake. This trail is not much traveled. Most everyone stops at the bluff. We came to the Stargate Keeper. Remember, it was the huge tree trunk, struck by lightning many years ago. Only its shell remained but it still towered with dignity, hollowed out by time, still beautiful. I heard a message clearly and stopped to take notice. *You are entering the Great Gateway OM, the point of origination. This is where you must leave all your baggage behind. If you are not pure of heart you may not enter.*

I share this message with Jim and we take a moment of silence to surrender the baggage we may be carrying with us. I had lots to leave behind. It had only been a few weeks since the end of our pilgrimage and already the physical world had a way of slowly creeping in, veiling our connection to pure Light. In this short time I had attracted some energetic debris and was ready to be "dusted off" as I call it. We continue walking. Apparently I had not surrendered it all. Ready to take a step I look down to see a small black snake with a yellow stripe down its back basking in the early morning sun. Startled, I jump back. "Well," said Jim, "I guess you didn't leave all your baggage behind." Yes, true. And so again I ask to leave behind all that is not of pure essence so I may enter this sacred spot. We continue on and come to the outcropping that resembles the Chief. Undeniable—his forehead, eyes, nose and mouth. I ask Jim if he got a picture of Chief on our last visit. "I tried," he answered, but like Mount Aneroid it was not to be captured on film.

We turn the corner to the clearing leading into the lake and there on the ground lay some newly chewed branches, remnants of a chipmunk's or squirrel's early morning breakfast I assumed. This is a small area, room for one or two people. One end leads into the lake, the other blocked by the Chief rock outcropping. We find the sacred *Gateway OM* where we buried the bundle. Untouched and undiscovered by the curious. It lies in a beautiful grotto. Chief's protecting it. We find a spot near the shore and spread our jackets out to sit. This time we brought crackers for the minnows and began delightfully feeding the little fish. It was very satisfying to see the flurry as they discovered this unexpected treat. The wildflowers carpeting the ground had long gone to seed. How quickly nature shows its splendor and then disappears.

We sit. And Jim nonchalantly asks, "What do you think those prints are?" I look over right next to where I am sitting and I see animal prints. Too big for a dog, not a cat, looks like a bear paw. "Looks like bear but too small," I say. "And only one; if it were a baby bear it would be with its mother and there would be more prints. It could be a two year old." "Yes," Jim says, "Probably a two-year-old." Then he slowly points out the chewed branches, the remainder of a few flower petals and fresh scat. Fresh! My alarms have been rung. I do not welcome coming face-to-face with a bear or even at a distance. My friend, Velvet, says the bear only shows up when you are ready. She, too, had a fear of bears. Then she was ready. She encountered the bear and now scampers freely through the woods unafraid. I can't say the same. Obviously, I am not ready to meet the bear. Jim proceeds to point out where the little bear spent the night, laying right on the *Gateway OM.* In his calm demeanor he remarks, "Good thing you left your baggage with the snake. This would have really released anything you were holding on to!" "In more ways than one" I reply. "Time to go!" And we're off.

THE LAST WORD

On your Journey OM pilgrimage you entered eternity, timelessness, a moment without time. You brought the past from 10,000 years ago, from 1877 to the present.

Chief Joseph

At home in Rancho Bernardo, we're settling in to a new reality. Every activity has taken on a prayerful tone, a majestic method. There is reverence in all we do, simple things like washing the car, shopping at the grocery store. We are in this world but not of it. How many times have we heard that saying and not really understood its meaning? We do now. We have been on a magic carpet ride neither of us could have imagined. And so we carry on with our daily routines back where we began.

This is my story. We all have a story. In Truth, each of our stories, is an illusion. It is not real as I think it. It is my story unique to me, one that triggered my emotional body and stimulated my mental body so I could learn the lessons I asked and needed to learn in this visit to this beautiful Planet Earth. If there is a piece of my story, or a part in my role in this play of life that will inspire your Truth and help you on your way back to the One, then it serves. If it makes you laugh and entertains you, then it serves.

The tapestry is woven: As Above, So Below—Heaven on Earth. Ten thousand years ago, 1877, Now to Infinity. We are each a unique color and texture, the threads of the warp and weft. Each of us is woven into the masterpiece; the tapestry not complete without our entwining. And that's what I've learned on this Stargate pilgrimage: my color and texture, my thread, my importance. You will be offered your pilgrimage and your gift will be the discovery of your color and texture, your thread, and your importance to God's masterpiece. We are One. We are integral. We are the whole and we are complete only with each other.

This journey ends as all journeys do. We are complete. We really have no idea what we did on a cosmic level. We know it was fun. We know it was an adventure. We know we took a trip. What we did through the eyes of God only He is aware. It does not matter. We were asked to be the Divine vessels for His

Will to flow through. That is all we were asked to do. Mission accomplished. Working with the Ascended Masters is a stair step effect. Each level has its own plateau and finale and integration and then we move to the next. We go through another passage, another initiation and another form of ignition into being a higher initiate. And in this way, in Love we Journey OM.

And now I sit waiting for the next "tap on the shoulder."

Journey OM

Joseph's Seed

By Judith K. Moore

I pray beside the banks
OF THE MIGHTY SALMON RIVER
Ancient Country on the Path of Chief Joseph
His journey for
FREEDOM FROM THE CHAINS OF OPPRESSION

OH! Gallant Warrior
Your spirit they could not chain
Your soul they could not capture
In my heart I can feel your song of
FREEDOM

My Feet immersed in this
River of life with yours
I Call to the WINDS
Return OH! Blessed one
Come to us from the Spirit Country
Journey here
To Mend THE HOOP

Bring to us your Spirit SEEDS
That we might
PLANT THEM DEEP WITHIN OUR SOULS
And water them with
TRUTH
And bless them with the
SUN OF HEALING LIGHT
That we might be your fertile Soil
SEEDS BURSTING FORTH
With Joseph's songs of
FREEDOM

I pray beside the banks of
THE MIGHTY SALMON RIVER
I open my eyes in time to see a mighty
EAGLE soars across the SUN
OH GALLANT JOSEPH—IS THAT YOU?
Coming home to
SPREAD THE SEEDS OF CHANGE
THAT OUR PEOPLE MAY LIVE[7]

---

[7] The poem, Joseph's Seeds was written by Judith in 1995 on a stop along Chief Joseph's trail. While praying beside the Salmon River not too far from Coyote Fishnet she felt the urge to look up, saw an Eagle, and intuited the spiritual connection to Chief Joseph. This poem was brought forward.

References

Andrews, Ted (1993) *Animal Speak.* United States: Llewellyn Worldwide Ltd.

Brady, Teresa, www.businesswritingediting.biz

Cota-Robles, Patricia Diane, (2007) *The Next Step...* Tucson, Arizona: New Age Study of Humanity's Purpose

Farmer, Steven (2006) *Animal Spirit Guides.* United States: Hay House, Inc.

Jones, Aurelia Louise. (2007) *The Seven Sacred Flames.* Mount Shasta, California: Mount Shasta Light Publishing

Moore, Judith K., *www.recordsofcreation.com*

Nerburn, Kent. (2005) *Chief Joseph and Flight of the Nez Perce.* San Francisco, California: Harper San Francisco, a Division of Harper Collins Publishers

Schroeder, W. (2005) *Ascended Masters & Their Retreats.* Mount Shasta, California: Ascended Master Teaching Foundation

Simmons, Robert and Ahsian, Naisha (2007) *The Book of Stones.* East Montpelier, Vermont: Heaven & Earth Publishing LLC

Stone, Joshua David. (1998) *The Easy-To-Read Encyclopedia of the Spiritual Path, Volumes, I, III, IV, VI, XI, XIV.* Sedona, Arizona: Light Technology Publishing

Towe, Dave, *www.beyondbodywork.com*

Vocare M.A., Ahriah, *SpiritShift@earthlink.net*

Wilfong, Cheryl. (2006) *Following the Nez Perce Trail.* Corvallis, Oregon: Oregon State University Press

In Gratitude

Journey OM is not one pen but a collaboration of several gifted individuals and spiritual masters coming together to record this story of the timely and powerful awakening to the ascension process.

I am forever grateful to you, my dear friend Judith K. Moore. You invited me and encouraged me to accept my "God job" and bring this work forward. Through you, Chief Joseph tapped me on the shoulder and requested I pick up where he left off. Your blessed connection to Source initiated the majesty of spiritual wisdom to put *Journey OM* into written words. Your life's dedication to being of service to the awakening of Heaven on Earth is a blessing for us all.

Teresa Brady, my friend "T" you are the counsel I count on for honesty and clarity. Our friendship spans seventeen years and a multitude of corporate adventures. Over time our paths have crossed and diverged, running parallel and polar.

Teresa you are my professional editor, legal beagle and Starbucks pal. *Journey OM* has your spirit written all over it; I thank you for crossing all the "t's" and opening my eyes.

Since I was born without a compass, God provided me with Jim Kelly, my beloved husband, companion and scout. Together we journeyed every step on this pilgrimage, over 4,000 miles, heart-to-heart in Love, laughter and awe. Through Jim's eyes the indescribable beauty of our pilgrimage was captured on film documenting this surreal journey. *Journey OM* is a Love story in more ways than One.

Thank you, Ahriah Vocare. You are a clear channel of the highest source of Ascended Master and Archangelic wisdom. You selflessly moved beyond your comfort zone to bring in the frequencies of Light necessary for me to embark on this pilgrimage. You have my eternal gratitude.

James G. Kelly IV, whether you are teaching the mastery and mystery of golf, expressing God's love as only a son, husband and father can, or expanding the beauty of life through your art, you are gifted with the visualization of creation in all you do. Thank you for bringing your vision of Chief Joseph to life in your divinely inspired drawings for Journey OM.

Thank you, Christi Masters. You gave me the most precious gift of all. Working with the Ascended Masters in faith and trust at a level neither of us could comprehend you opened the Universal Gateways in my physical body through your ascended mastery of acupuncture.

Thank you, Dave Towe for the sacred ash of the Native American Nations and the Mother Stone from Isis herself. Thank you, Bill Kniceley for the holy water from Lourdes and thank you Randy and Judith for the miraculous soil of Chimayo. To my earth and soul families and friends, those too many to name, and you know who you are; from my heart to your heart I express my deepest Love and appreciation.

To my teachers past and present: Spiritual Masters, Chief Joseph, St. Germain, Archangel Michael and Gabriel, Lord Melchizedek, Lord Maitreya, Babaji, Mataji and Osho and all the unnamed angels and ancient ancestor star beings known and unknown who led me to this point of ascension, who directed me to say "Yes" to my destiny—I love YOU.

Most humbly and lovingly I thank you, Lord Sananda and Lady Nada for walking hand-in-hand with me on this earthly plane and endowing me with the privilege of being your chela and the Divine vessel for Thy Will to flow through.

About the Author: Shima Shanti

Life's experiences have touched Shima Shanti in profound and unexpected ways. During her careers as a corporate executive and then an entrepreneur, the vision of a *future memory* led Shima to realize the world is ascending to a higher vibrational consciousness. As she gracefully opens to enlightenment, Shima has been deepening her understanding of the ascension process through gifted resources, intense study, and insight from the Spiritual realms.

On her path of self-discovery, she came to know her God Presence embodied in her physical being. Realizing she was no longer bound by old karmic patterns, she found her Spiritual freedom and embarked on her path of service as an ascension way-shower.

Since then, Shima has answered Spirit's call to adventure, traveling the Western United States, Canada, Portugal, and

Spain. She has followed both established pilgrimage routes and spiritual retreats, including Chief Joseph's Trail, Archangel Michael's etheric Temple of Faith, and the *Camino de Santiago de Compostela*. Each journey has deepened Shima's self-realization of God.

Of these travels, nothing was more profound than her walk through Portugal and Spain in 2012. Alone, in a foreign country, with nothing but a backpack and herself, she walked nearly 500 kilometers in unyielding rain. That's when she accepted the challenge to fully surrender to *All That Is*. The heart-searching solitude she experienced gave her a clear understanding of her Divine purpose. It has evolved into her own *Camino*—and her next call to serve.

Shima's soon-to-be published book is the revelation of Truth and unveiled mystery told through her *Camino* journey. As this Light-minded soul says, "I'm always ready for the next tap on the shoulder to serve."

The author has been writing creatively for more than 20 years. With her husband of 35 years, she and Jim balance their lives between San Diego, California, and Whitefish, Montana, contrasting walks on the beach with hikes in the high mountains. They fully savor the simple actions of life through the enthusiasm of their grandson Micah and their Maltese pup Star.

Also By Shima Shanti

The Soul Journeyer's Companion

A Cosmic-Rememoir

Book II of the Journey OM Series

Hats I Am

A Children's Book

Ascension Kis

Opening the Doorways to Light

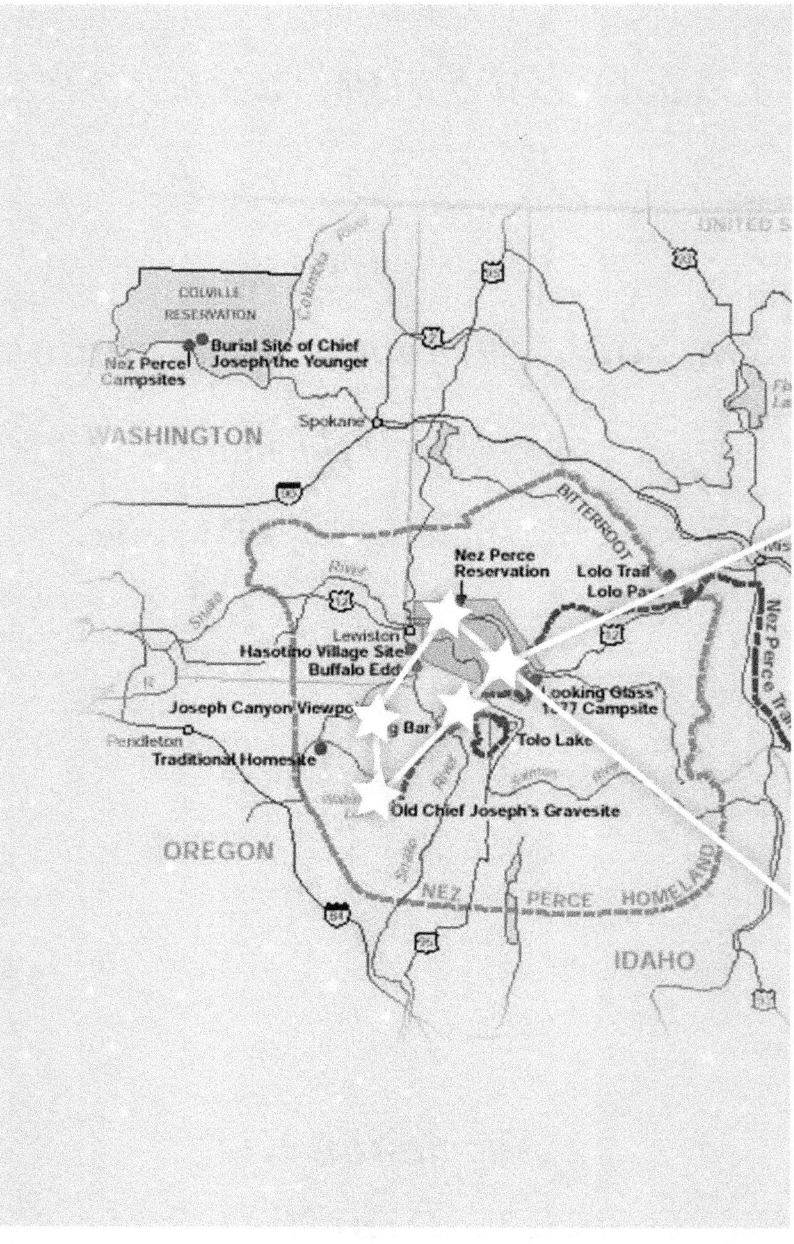
COLVILLE RESERVATION
Burial Site of Chief Joseph the Younger
Nez Perce Campsites
Spokane
WASHINGTON
BITTERROOT
Nez Perce Reservation
Lolo Trail
Lewiston
Hasotino Village Site
Joseph Canyon Viewpo
Looking Glass 1877 Campsite
Pendleton
Tolo Lake
Traditional Homesite
Old Chief Joseph's Gravesite
OREGON
NEZ PERCE HOMELAND
IDAHO

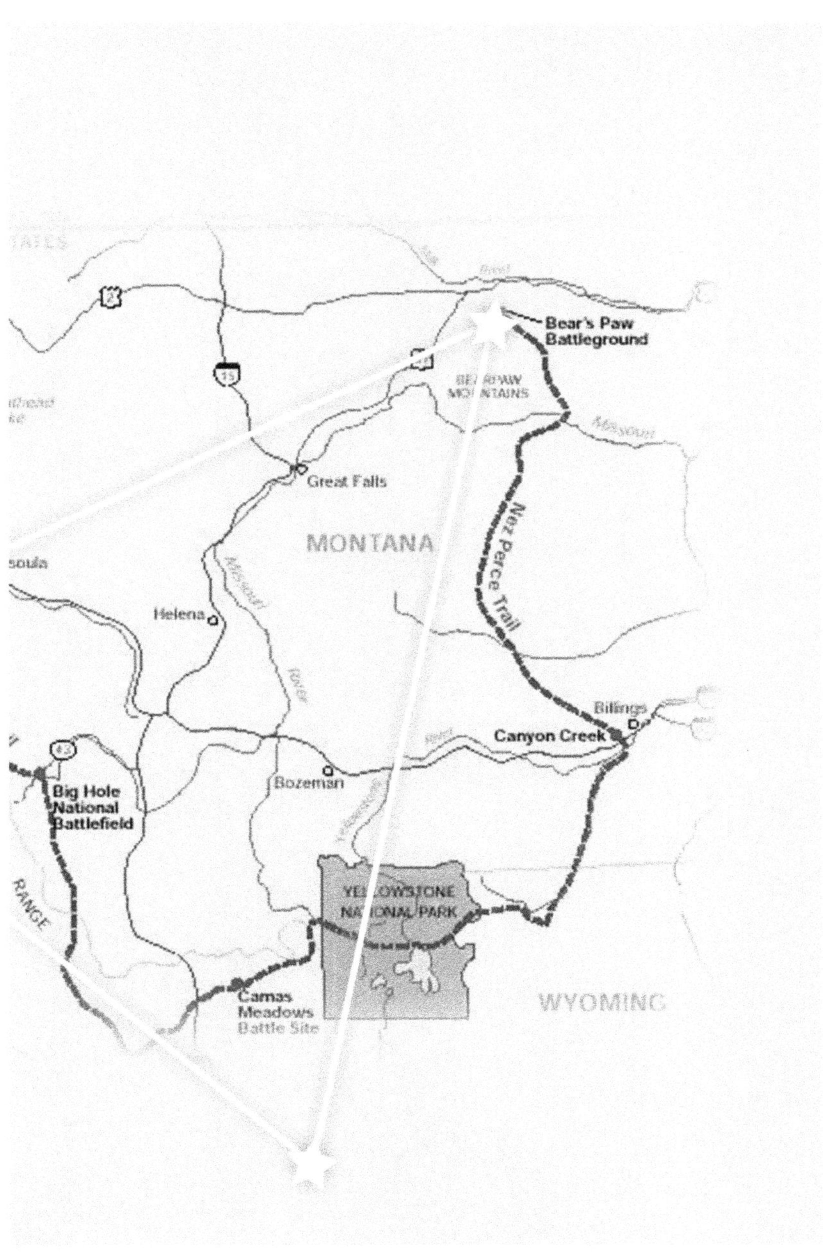
Bear's Paw
Battleground
MONTANA
Great Falls
Helena
Bozeman
Billings
Canyon Creek
Nez Perce Trail
Big Hole
National
Battlefield
YELLOWSTONE
NATIONAL PARK
Camas
Meadows
Battle Site
WYOMING
RANGE

www.ingramcontent.com/pod-product-compliance
Lightning Source LLC
Chambersburg PA
CBHW031831090426
42741CB00005B/208

* 9 7 8 0 9 9 1 5 4 8 1 2 5 *